D0756835

Shredding The Shame

Shredding The Shame

Healing Childhood Abuse

Kelli Benis

First Published in Canada 2014 by Influence Publishing

Book Cover Design: Marla Thompson
Typeset: Greg Salisbury
Author Photographer: Sara Novak

DISCLAIMER: This book is a work of Non-Fiction. Some of the names of characters in this book have been changed to protect their anonymity.

~

Library and Archives Canada Cataloguing in Publication

Benis, Kelli, 1969-, author
    Shredding the shame : healing childhood abuse / Kelli Benis.

ISBN 978-1-77141-059-5 (pbk.)

1. Benis, Kelli, 1969-. 2. Adult child sexual abuse victims--Mental health. 3. Adult child sexual abuse victims--Rehabilitation. 4. Adult child sexual abuse victims--Canada--Biography. I. Title.

RC569.5.A28B36 2014   616.85'83690651   C2014-904726-6

To all the victims who have been silenced—
know that you are not alone, together we have a voice.

Testimonials

"Kelli has transformed her life from what could have become a lifelong struggle into a life of tearing down the rear-view mirror and investing her passion to help others achieve the same to say 'I DID.'"
Colin Harms, Founder, I DID Brand

"Raising her voice to help other victims of abuse find theirs—Benis has written a book that is brave, honest and inspirational. She shows that however traumatic our experiences may have been, we can heal and break free from the shackles of the past. Perhaps the book's greatest gift is its powerful message to victims of abuse that they are not alone."
Glori Meldrum, Founder and Chair, Little Warriors

"An insightful recounting of a year where Benis' healing journey is punctuated by synchronous events that highlight the power of shedding the shame associated with child sexual abuse. A story of courage and the strength of community."
Cynthia Bland, President, Voice Found

"It takes great courage to heal our past trauma, to break the chains of shame and use our life experiences for good. Kelli Benis is one divinely courageous woman. Her determination to heal runs deep in her veins and her passion to inspire and empower others is palpable."
Sue Dumais, Author of *Heart Led Living—When Hard Work Becomes Heart Work*

"We are happy for Kelli as she finds empowerment on her healing path. May she continue to inspire others and have many more healing conversations along her journey."
Kim Barthel and Theo Fleury, Authors of *Conversations With a Rattlesnake*

Acknowledgements

Lou, thank you for taking on double duty at work and home so that I could bring this story to life. Your support, love and encouragement have meant more to me than words can ever express. My heart, you hold forever, I love you madly.

Ali and Tony, thank you for the countless hours spent listening to me, for your support and encouragement, and for loving me just the way I am. I couldn't have been blessed with more loving kids.

Devany and Connor, thank you for accepting me into your world with open arms and loving me even though you didn't have to.

Mom and Dad, thank you for providing me with an unshakeable foundation, endless hugs, bottomless love, and the ability to find humour in any situation. From the moment you brought me home from "the finance company" I have loved you.

Theo Fleury, the inspiration you provided at the Victor Walk and every time I have heard you speak since, have shown me what true courage looks like and reminded me of the power of one voice.

Glori Meldrum, you have shown me that anything is possible if you set your mind to it. Thank you for welcoming me with open arms and showing me how powerful a dream can be.

Julie Salisbury, thank you for helping me to sort the bits and find the flow, and for helping me to know where to place my first step, and the next and the next. I'm right chuffed to know you.

Gulnar, Lyda, Alina, Nina, and Greg at Influence Publishing, thank you for the care that you took in getting this story out in a way that reflected my intentions and for never once being too busy to answer my endless questions and guide me through this process.

Torre Truba, I will always be grateful for your steady encouragement and friendship. You are an honest voice and your strength is immeasurable.

Alison Lee, thank you for the road trips, the memories, and the knowledge that you can make a difference no matter how young or old you are.

Heather and Shane Lee, you have raised a bright, intelligent, courageous young woman who will no doubt help to make this world a better place—thank you for that.

Contents

Preface

I was sexually abused by my grandfather from the time I was four up until I was twelve. This book is not about the abuse I suffered. It is about how it took me forty years to come to terms with that abuse and how my whole life now is about helping others who have suffered similar traumatic childhoods.

When I started writing this book several years ago, I focused mostly on my abuse and the difficulties that I had faced in life as a result of that abuse. That just didn't feel right to me anymore; it was also very hard to do and often left me feeling as though I was reliving the horrors of my past, over and over. I really wasn't too thrilled about writing about my pain just so that someone else could pick up the book and feel comforted by it in the same way that the saying "misery loves company" works. I really wondered what would be the purpose of doing that now. Who would it help? I think that I was trying to somehow let people who had never experienced abuse have a peek into my life and gain a greater understanding of what that kind of abuse does to a child and how it follows them through their whole life.

When I returned to writing my book in 2013, I chose to write my story from a place of healing. The abuse had long since stopped and I refused to allow it to keep me clutched in its grip. The story that now interested me was the story of a girl who looked her past straight in the eye and said, "Your story stops here; I'm moving on without you."

Those who will be inspired by this book already understand the pain, isolation, and the devastating effect that abuse has in their lives. To point that out again to you, the reader, would be redundant. What we as survivors need more than anything is to know that we are not alone and that there is an opportunity for us all to enjoy full and happy lives.

I have always said that the point of adversity is not so that you can one day get past it all and look back and think, "Man, I got through that; aren't I special!" At the end of our lives there will not be a big room full of plaques engraved with each of our personal adversities that we have overcome. That simply is not what life is about.

The adversities that we face and how we overcome them provide us with tools that will help us reach out to others who are in similar situations. The greatest gifts we receive are the ones that we in turn give to someone else. I feel life is about recognizing that we all need a helping hand at some point and the goal is to reach out that hand to others, however you can and as often as you can. We do not need degrees or titles or money or fame to be able to make a difference. All that we need to lessen someone else's suffering is to be true to ourselves and to do what we can, however we are able.

I used to think that I needed something special, something more than I already had, in order to make a difference. I now know that each and every one of us has the power to make a difference; all we need is a desire to do so and then the guts to act on that desire. We can no longer wait for someone else to take the lead. We must trust in our own abilities and be proud of ourselves for the courage that it takes to act, to try our best at making lives better.

The events I write about in this book took place over a period of one year, one year that was filled with new experiences that opened both my eyes and my heart. These are the moments, the memories, and the insights that these new experiences provided me with. They have since shown me that one voice does make a difference and that when we believe in ourselves, anything is possible; and when we believe in others, that is when we can expect the miracles to happen.

Never underestimate the power of one voice and the power that you have in healing yourself. You alone hold the key to your freedom; all you have to do is use it.

Chapter One

Victors Unite

Standing on the steps of Parliament Hill in Ottawa, surrounded by a sea of Victors all wearing orange, I look up at the buildings around us, the flags waving in the breeze, the sound of the voices mingling, and I feel the magnificence of it all. Never in my life could I have dreamed of a more perfect ending to the shame that I have suffered in silence for so long. The gently falling, light misting rain lands on my face and washes away my solitude. I am not alone and I know that I never really will be again. Here I am surrounded by relative strangers, and yet the bonds we have forged through our mutual suffering and excruciating silence can never be broken and for that I am eternally grateful. Never before had I given any thought as to what it would feel like to break free from that solitude and isolation. Even if I had, I could not have imagined the overwhelming relief it would provide. In that moment, in the shadow of the Peace Tower, our secrets all became our stories, and we wore them proudly like badges of honour.

This was May 23, 2013.

I took my time mentally going over all that was happening in order to commit the events of that day to my permanent memory, never wanting to forget a single moment of it. I recall leaving our hotel after having our breakfast with Alex Vorobej, Vice President of Voice Found, "A Canadian non-profit organization that is committed to the prevention of Child Sexual Abuse and supporting adult survivors." I recall how all of us had been totally excited to meet up with Theo Fleury and his team for the Orange Movement Victor Walk for survivors of child sexual abuse on the steps leading up to Canada's Parliament Building. I recall how we had a fair bit of time to kill before he and his team would arrive, so we thought we should walk the route and see if we could meet up and walk a distance with them. I recall how we walked the streets of Ottawa, all wearing our bright orange Victor shirts, and carrying the posters that Alison, a fifteen-year-old vocal advocate from Lethbridge who was travelling with us, had made at the airport.

I recall how, shortly after we started out on our venture near Parliament Hill, the clouds opened and dumped buckets of water on us. We were soaked, I mean really soaked! None of us cared though; it would have taken more than rain to dampen our spirits. I smiled to myself remembering how, while waiting at the crosswalk for the lights to change, a car drove through a monster puddle left over from the previous cloudburst, and drenched Heather. I couldn't help but laugh as I watched the puddle come up like a tidal wave in slow motion to soak her. Heck! All anyone could do was laugh, and so laugh we did.

I recall how I spent the next hour or so trying to guess which way Theo and his team would be coming up to Parliament, and then looking for them all up and down the streets that we ventured along. My heart is warm as I remember the new friends that we made when we set out to find the group; we ran into two ladies who were also there for the Victor Walk. I recall being surprised by the level of relief I felt in seeing those two, knowing there would be more than just Brian, our new friend and fellow Victor whom we'd met at the hotel the evening before, and us on the steps with Theo.

I have since reflected on the stories that we shared with each other along with the special connection we felt toward each other, which could not be dismissed, and how we then promised to make sure we stayed in touch once the walk was over. I thought about Christine, another fellow Victor, and how she mentioned she was also writing a book and that we should keep in touch and encourage and support each other any way that we could.

I stood there gazing up at the Peace Tower and everything

around me and hoped that these events would remain with me as memories once I left this shredding ground, and that the shame that would be thrown down and cast away that day would forever remain nothing more than a distant memory to those who had shred it.

Through all the time walking around, I was filled with excitement and a feeling of being utterly determined to end my silence and of wanting to be a voice for those who could not yet use theirs. I felt like we were representing all the survivors who could not be there and all the victims who felt alone and were still struggling through abuse every single day. I remember so badly wanting to shout out and let them know they are not alone; they have nothing to be ashamed of; they will be okay.

I felt such incredible gratitude toward my mom for her relentless support and encouragement. Having her by my side, giving me hugs, and her laughing with me as we were on that journey are some of the most cherished memories that I have. Together, we were breaking the silence and making a difference and, oh how badly I wished that everyone in the world who has ever suffered at the hands of another could feel what I was feeling that day: hope, gratitude, love, and a surreal sense of calm, peace, and joy.

I thought back about how we had been searching and then eventually met up with Theo and his team behind the Justice Building, which was about three blocks away from the steps of Parliament Hill. I was immediately relieved to see that we were not alone; there was a big group of people and each person was wearing orange.

It all seems a distant memory now, like a dream that fades with the morning light. I desperately etched each memory and the emotion that was attached to it into my brain where I could hold it safely and where I could pull it out for a source of encouragement in the future, should the road ever get rocky. I remember the awe I felt in seeing there were camera crews, news crews, and reporters mixed in with the crowd. I recall the taste of my tears as they flowed down my face when we made our way toward the group, and how I tried so hard to hold them back. For once, the tears I held back were not tears of sadness, but rather tears of joy and relief and pride. The memories I had of the past forty years had made me feel so terribly alone; there on Parliament Hill I finally felt like I belonged; never again will I feel alone; we were united.

I savour the memory of being introduced to Theo by Alison, who had met him previously at a fundraising event for Little Warriors, a national charitable organization based in Canada, which focuses on education and prevention of child sexual abuse. I must admit, I remember thinking it was pretty cool to have her introduce us to him. In that one moment, he became the hero that I never really had growing up. I couldn't help but wonder what would happen in the future since Alison had taken that opportunity to ask Theo if he would be coming to light her tree in December and he said that he would. Even though at that time I remember thinking how cool that would be, yet truly not thinking it would actually end up happening. The smile on Alison's face was enough to light up the rainy city as Theo signed Alison's poster that said, "I Am Brave" with "To Alison, Don't Quit Before The Miracle. You Are Brave." He signed his autograph and wrote underneath, "Victor Walk, May 23, 2013, Parliament Hill."

It occurred to me how odd it was that I had not thought to bring something for Theo to sign. I mean this is a pretty famous guy! I guess I figured that, for me, what Theo represents is a courageous individual who is passionate about helping others. I knew who he is and all that he had done through his international hockey career, but that just didn't matter at all to me. He is so down to earth, such a straight shooter about his abuse, and he genuinely cares about everyone.

What struck me was the way everyone had wanted to speak to Theo and share his or her story with him. As they thanked him for being a voice for all of us who have survived abuse, he accepted those thanks with such humility. It didn't matter how long the press was waiting for Theo; he put all his attention directly on the person who was in front of him and he offered words of encouragement and acceptance to every single person he met. Hugs were given freely and often, and most importantly, they were genuine; there is no doubt that the recipients of those hugs would remember them for the remaining days of their lives, and they would be stored as part of the new memories of happiness and acceptance that would replace the old worn-out memories of anger and isolation.

I cherish the memory of our walk toward the steps of the Parliament Building. We were separated from Theo, but I am pretty sure that he could hear Alison singing Theo's anthem "Walk With Thousands" (www.youtube.com/watch?v=aFvc7WvkLqY) the whole way there. The feeling of being so overwhelmed with emotions, filled with happiness, determination, relief, and love still rings strongly in my mind and resonates with my soul. For years, I had stuffed my emotions down so deeply that they could not be found, and now they were bubbling up and I truly felt like I could and would make a difference. I had been called, and I will honour that calling any, and every, way that I can. I recall my mom saying, "This is it, Kelli. This is the reason for it all. I'm so proud of you." Her voice dances in my mind and lifts my heart.

Mom was right. In this one day, my entire past had provided me with my new purpose in life: I would be the voice for the voiceless, a beacon of light for so many of our "lost" children. It was on that day that I truly felt gratitude for every bit of my abuse and every bit of adversity that has crossed my path. All I had gone through in life up to that point had been put in front of me to prepare me for what I would need in order to help others overcome the same obstacles. I would not trade one second of my past for anything. I am here because of where I've been and what I have experienced; without all that, I would not be in a position to help anyone else.

Life is full of challenges. Overcoming them is only half the equation. It is what we do once we overcome the challenges that will define us and help us to leave this world a better place than the way we found it. Small glimpses of the possibilities for the future dared to dance in and out of my consciousness, apparently waiting for me to pluck them out of my mind and turn them into reality.

The events of that day as I stood on the steps of Parliament Hill surrounded by fellow Victors play through my mind now like a movie in slow motion. I can replay how Theo addressed the crowd and how he offered words of encouragement and strength. One thing he said stuck with me. He said that we each need to find our voice and speak up. He understood that sometimes we are scared and ashamed, but the shame is not ours to carry; it is our abusers'. He promised us that nothing that might happen as a result of speaking up could ever be worse than everything we had been through at the hands of our abusers and already survived.

The statistics roll through my brain. We are not alone. One in three girls and one in six boys are victims of child sexual abuse in Canada according to a report from 1984. The numbers are staggering and it is time that we heard them.

Theo explained to everyone the reason he called the walk the Victor Walk was that each of us had survived and by shedding the shame, by finding our voices, we could feel we are no longer victims; we are Victors.

The mascot for the walk was a pretty cool frog; his name is Victor. Theo's story for the reason the mascot is a frog was pretty cool as well. He spoke of how when he was healing, he connected with his roots as a Métis Aboriginal Canadian. A young spiritual leader had asked Theo if he would like to go on a hike with him. The twenty-three-year-old spiritual leader took Theo into the mountains. They climbed up and up until they reached a clearing that had a whole bunch of animal carvings, and the young leader started to explain what the animal was and what each carving meant. Theo just happened to be standing over the carving of a frog. The leader asked Theo if he had ever seen a frog hop backwards. Theo said that no he hadn't and the spiritual leader said that the frog can look to the left and look to the right, but the frog is always going straight ahead.

Theo then told us he'd said, "Well, that's me! I'm going that way, forward. I don't want to go back the other way. It's too painful back there and I don't want to live back there anymore. I want to just keep going forward."

Then, fast forward nine months later, he was in Winnipeg speaking at another conference. There is a sweat lodge on Main Street in Winnipeg; Theo explained that a sweat lodge is a place to go and heal. During the sweat lodge ceremony—a very spiritual event—aboriginal people build a fire outside and put a bunch of rocks in this fire. They then dig a hole in the ground and build a frame around it made out of birch, which is really bendy, and then they cover the frame with cloth. The heated rocks are put in the hole and water is poured over the rocks; steam rises up and then flows down the walls of the lodge. This is very cleansing. Aboriginals use herbs and all sorts of natural medicines.

So Theo did a sweat lodge ceremony, and it was like every other sweat that he had ever done: it was wonderful and spiritual.

The next day he spoke to a group and told the story of the frog. As soon as he was done speaking, the spiritual leader, who had run the sweat the night before, grabbed the microphone from him and said, "You'll never guess what walked into the sweat lodge last night. I couldn't explain it. I saw this spirit walk into the sweat lodge, but didn't know what it was about. A frog walked into the sweat lodge last night."

Theo said he was thinking, "Wow, now that is really cool! Now this frog story is starting to gain some momentum. It is starting to mean more and more." He said that it had happened again, the next time he was in Calgary, when he was speaking to the

Meadow Lake Tribal Council. There were eight different bands there, so again he told the story of the frog and one of the elders went up to him after the speech and said, "Did you know that the frog is the healer of children?"

Theo said he just about fell over. He went on to explain that everywhere he goes, there is a frog. He would check into a hotel room in Halifax and right beside the nightstand there would be a frog. So, when they were making the plans for the Victor Walk, they thought they should have something that would represent the walk, because it wasn't about him anymore, and so they chose the frog. And because we call ourselves Victors, they named the frog "Victor the Frog."

Theo said what he feels the frog means to us is that no matter what we have been through in life, it's about getting up every morning and putting one foot in front of the other. It's about taking baby steps, because the frog doesn't get too far with just one jump. He just keeps going ahead and going ahead, forward and forward and forward, and for all of us who are survivors, that is such an important thing to remember. Every day when we get up, we just put one foot in front of the other and take baby steps, because if we get too far ahead of ourselves, we get into trouble and if we start going backwards, then we get into trouble too. So let's just keep taking baby steps and baby steps forward.

Theo spoke about how miracles happen every day for us who are in this, because when you see people get rid of shame right in front of you, it is absolutely the most incredible gift you will ever receive in your life.

I watched as Theo greeted victim after victim, listening to each of their stories and thanking them for having the courage to stand up and tell those stories. I am quite sure he must have been totally exhausted, both physically and emotionally, after that day, but he never once let it show.

I watched as two people were reunited on those steps; they had not seen each other for years. They grew up as children living right next door to each other, each suffering the pain of being sexually abused all alone, and never knowing that the other was suffering through the same kind of abuse. It was not until they saw each other there on the steps of the Parliament Building that they found out about the other's abuse. They talked quietly to each other the whole time they were together there on those steps, and they held hands throughout their conversation. Scrolling through my pictures from that day, I realize I have photos of them I didn't know they were in. What a beautiful reunion! It served as a reminder to me of just how many people have suffered in silence and felt like they were all alone, but actually could be living right next door to someone who was also suffering the same fate.

As I walked with my mom away from the crowd and Theo, and headed back to the hotel, I could feel the significance of it all. This would be the beginning of the end to the reign that our shame had held over us. It was now our turn to shred any of the remaining shame, kick it to the curb, and begin the rest of our lives enjoying the relief that comes after you finally stop carrying such a heavy load. I felt there would be, quite simply, no way to go on living the way I had lived before the walk, and no way to ignore all the people suffering around me in silence.

My mind rolled over and over the thoughts, feelings, emotions, and personal victories from the day, and I savoured each and every one of them. I am a Victor, part of a larger community that will continue to grow in numbers daily, and I will begin to explore just how I fit into this larger picture, and how I will contribute to this new community. As we each summon the courage to find our voices, I think many other Victors will find new and exciting ways that they are able to inspire others and make changes in whatever ways their fields of expertise allow them to.

Feeling just as inspired as me, my mom kept the conversation going while hanging onto each new feeling we had encountered.

"Isn't it neat how this all came together? We have to follow through with sharing what we have learned today. How amazing that we were so determined to attend the walk today. Someone is watching over us and guiding us for sure!

"I am so thankful you were able to find a way to have Alison and her mom Heather, here with us. I think they needed this as much as we did and experiencing this will give us all the motivation to bring the issue of child sexual abuse to light. I think it is great how Alison has connected with Little Warriors and has been able to take part in their ad campaign and help build the Be Brave Ranch. How incredible that she had the courage to stand up and raise awareness and money for the ranch through selling her light bulb sponsorships last year. Imagine the number of people that she touched if she was able to raise almost $10,000 with that initiative and do it all at the age of fifteen. It's truly inspiring.

"I really hope that we can somehow connect with organizations like Little Warriors and Voice Found; I think there might be opportunities for us to help them out. We need to contact them as soon as we get home."

Her thoughts poured out of her one after another without her even taking a pause to breathe.

I totally agreed with Mom. This had all happened so fast, really. One day we were talking on the phone about making a difference and wondering just how we were going to be able to do that, and in a matter of a few short weeks, we had plunged head first into the centre of the Victor Movement. Neither of us had anticipated the whirlwind of events that had led us to that moment. We had simply taken a step, and that step had led us to the next one, and before we knew it we had felt empowered with the knowledge that even though we were only two people, we had the power to make a difference in the lives of so many. Our goal had been to help even just one person feel less alone and now here we were standing on the edge of a massive chasm of healing and we had only just begun.

The henna tattoos of Victor the Frog, which we wore proudly

on our forearms, served as symbols of our vow to elevate the conversation around child sexual abuse. The frogs reminded us of a time, not so long before, when we had a hard time even speaking the words "child sexual abuse" out loud; we lived our lives in ignorance of the magnitude of the epidemic that it is, and the trail of destruction it leaves in its wake. It forced me to think about how even though I myself had lived my childhood facing sexual abuse, I had remained oblivious to the statistics and the people those numbers represent. If I was unaware and yet I was a victim, how would the rest of the world become aware? How would changes be made if even the victims themselves didn't know how often it was occurring? Now there we were, with the frogs out in plain view for the whole world to see, exactly the way we want it to be.

I recall all the horror stories I'd heard in the last few weeks leading up to the walk, and at the walk itself, about how children who find the courage to speak up are often not believed, and how others watch as their abusers serve very little time in jail, or worse yet, how the abusers walk away without any convictions at all. Some of the victims had shared how they had felt devastated when their loved ones or the authorities did not believe them when they disclosed their abuse. Others spoke about how they had not been able to afford counselling and therapy, and were bumped out of the free mental health services offered, because their abusers had been court ordered to receive treatment and that took priority over the victims being treated.

I truly was shocked at the level of dysfunction that became apparent in our social systems. How can it be that such catastrophic levels of devastation happen every single day, and yet they are shrouded in silence with the victims being left to feel insignificant, less than a blip on the public radar? I know how: through shame and silence! I now know that if things are going to change it will have to start here, by ending the shame and silence, by speaking up, and by finding our voices, one by one.

It was that shame and silence that had allowed me to try to cling to some sort of a normal life following my abuse. This was the same shame and silence that fooled me into putting my head in the sand and go on thinking this was something that had happened to me and not really anyone else. This was the same shame and silence that allowed me and my family to sidestep the reality of what had happened right under our own roof and threatened to end the illusion of the picture-perfect life we showed to our neighbours and friends. I had chosen to handle my abuse that way, chosen to attempt to walk away from the reality of it, rather than to seek out justice for the heinous crimes that had been committed against me. We were a good, hardworking family. Our family name had never been dragged through the mud. My parents had worked hard at protecting me and my brother from the cruel and sickening crimes of the world, and yet, without knowing it, we were all affected by those crimes just the same.

The choice I had made was a reflection of the way I had dealt with the trauma as a child, not out of a conscious decision so much, but out of a need to survive and keep living any way that I could. The way I was able to make it this far was to jump back up like I was okay, like I was not affected by it at all. The rest of my life was normal and happy, and there was no way I could risk that normalcy by laying my pain out there for all to see. It wasn't bravery or any act of toughness that allowed me to do that; it was only my instinctual reaction to it and self-preservation that had allowed me to carry on.

Now the cat was out of the bag and I could see that my life did not come to a screeching halt because of it—it only got better—and the excuses that I had used to silence myself earlier were bullshit. Once again, I found myself singing the song "Girl On Fire" by Alicia Keys; it had played in my head often since Torre had put together the YouTube video (www.youtube.com/watch?v=4OXSve7eaeM) for me a few weeks earlier. It is my own personal anthem: when I listen to it or sing it, I feel strong. The video Torre made was the first real public version of my story. It was a shortened version, but the first public one regardless, and although it was awkward at first to watch it, I grew proud of it and my resilience.

As it turned out, our timing was perfect, and Mom and I got back to the hotel just in time to be greeted by my Uncle Bob. Our trip to Ottawa served a dual purpose for Mom and me. We planned to spend a few days with my Uncle Bob and Auntie Glo following the Victor Walk, since they live in Bath, Ontario, and it had been a few years since I had seen them. My aunt had been sick and was just finishing up her radiation treatments when she fell and broke her arm. Bob was thrilled that his sister and, dare I say, his "favourite niece" would be visiting.

Bob came to Ottawa and whisked us off to his place in Bath shortly after the walk ended. Still high with the newfound courage and determination that was coursing through my veins from the Victor Walk, I proceeded to talk my uncle's ear off the whole way to Bath. Bob is a very successful, retired businessman and he has a heart of gold.

When my grandfather, who was my abuser, had died years earlier, Bob had been my anchor and support, and we had developed a bond that would leave me feeling like we had never been apart, no matter how many years it was between visits. We talked about the Victor Walk and Little Warriors, and how it was so incredibly important to start raising awareness for this cause. We talked about how common child sexual abuse is, and how people who have experienced it often have a very hard time coming forward and speaking out about the abuse that they endured. He was really taken aback about the statistics and how often child sexual abuse occurs.

We talked about the shame I had felt, and quite frankly, my family had felt, and why we chose not to press charges, and decided to remain quiet about what had happened. I explained my reasons for not telling my parents when the abuse first happened.

I tried the best I could to relay to him the thought processes I had had as a child, the concern I had over hurting my mom, and the worry that if I spoke up back then, my life, which was otherwise perfect, would be reduced to one of chaos and endless court battles that would involve me being just as much on trial as my abuser.

We talked about the insignificant sentences our judicial system hands down to offenders in the unlikely event that a child is courageous enough to come forward, and how that, as we get older and realize how flawed the system is, it is even harder to speak up. People who are victims and the families of those victims often just want to move on with life and pretend the whole horrific mess of their past had not happened.

For me, I was given the choice to proceed in whatever way I felt I needed to, and I knew that I would have my family's support either way. Back then, when I told my parents, some twenty years earlier, I was still under the mind set of "I'm okay; I'm okay," and I was determined to barrel through it and get on with life. I had never played the "poor me" card and a part of me was afraid that, if I charged my grandfather, I would have a hard time maintaining my composure and outward happy appearance. It also meant that I would need to stand up to my grandfather, face him in court, and deal with knowing that I had put him behind bars, if in fact I actually won my case.

We discussed how even though what he had done to me, and no doubt other children, was unthinkable, he was still my grandfather and a part of me loved him. That was very hard for me to come to terms with; I pitied him and his inability to acknowledge that what he had done was wrong and would affect me for the rest of my life, in some way or another. I could almost forgive him, because he just wasn't wired right. Mind you, I must admit, any forgiveness I had given him was not enough to keep me from wishing he would spend the rest of his days alone and rejected. I wanted him to feel what I had felt growing up; I wanted revenge for my lost innocence as a child.

14

When he died, I was comforted by the fact that he died alone and felt so much relief in knowing that he couldn't hurt anyone ever again.

Uncle Bob was a retired Rotarian and, because I was currently a Rotarian, much of what we discussed in that regard was easily understood between us. I talked with him about how the district conference I had been to, with the RYLA (Rotary Youth Leadership Awards) students attending as guests in March 2013, had opened my eyes to just how much our youth need help today. We discussed at length how Rotarians would undertake such incredible projects all over the world and provide enormous amounts of money to those projects, which include everything from building schools to eradicating polio; but for Rotary projects here in Canada, we tend to stick to things like building playgrounds and art centres. I couldn't help but think how much of an impact there would be if we could educate Rotarians across Canada about the epidemic levels of child sexual abuse happening right in their own backyards.

You see, things like child sexual abuse are thought to happen in other places, not in Canada. And, it is also thought that if it is happening in Canada, it certainly would be among the underprivileged in our society, and not in the mainstream where the outstanding citizens are. If only that were true. If only.

The truth of the matter is that it happens everywhere and the perpetrators are often highly regarded in our communities; they are teachers, youth group leaders, councillors, church leaders, painters, funeral home directors, doctors, lawyers, and candlestick makers. There is no one set template for the face of an abuser. They are very good at what they do and very good at gaining the trust of those around them. Unfortunately, that also makes coming forward about the abuse very hard as well.

How does a child find the courage to blow the whistle on someone whom everybody else considers to be an awesome person? Why would anyone believe them? Parents teach children that pedophiles are creepy men wearing long trench coats and hiding in the bushes at the park or lurking in dark alleyways. The children know differently.

Bob couldn't believe that something, which occurs so commonly, is so rarely talked about and that there are no long-term healing centres for the children who fall victim to this. We both decided that something needs to be done to change that and agreed we would help each other any way we can to that end.

The morning following the Victor Walk, I awoke in Bob's beautiful home and made my way downstairs for a much-needed cup of coffee. I checked my Facebook account. My daughter Ali, who had been given permission to attend the Victor Walk in Lethbridge, which meant that she would miss class, had sent me a photo of the front page of our local newspaper *The Lethbridge Herald* as proof that she really went on the walk and didn't just bail on class and hang out at the mall. There it was in front of me: a photo of all my people—my husband, daughter, friend, brother-in-law, and sister-in-law—all braving the rain to support me and other Victors by walking in the Lethbridge Victor Walk.

What an incredible feeling to have that kind of support! It seemed like I was just coming back to earth from the excitement the day before and now, there I was, flying high once again, feeling overwhelming love and support from across the country. It really doesn't get any better than that, in my books!

THE TAKEAWAY LESSON

What is it that pulls at the core of your being? It is pulling for a reason, giving you a clue about how to learn something about yourself that you didn't know, or even showing you a way to take action around something that you are passionate about. We all have different desires, goals, passions, and challenges. So tune into yourself and listen carefully to what you learn. Don't be afraid to take action; thoughts and dreams alone will not provide results.

Chapter Two

Sister Stephanie

I am so thankful for the family I have; every single person in it has offered me emotional support and unconditional love. My cousin Michael made the trek to Bath from Woodstock to have a visit with my mom and me while we were in the area. His plans to come to Bob's had been delayed a few days and I was anxious to see him again. This trip of ours had so many things mixed into it and all of them were exciting. I had attended the Victor Walk, spent some much needed time with Bob and Glo, was looking forward to seeing Michael again, and, if that wasn't enough, I was also planning on meeting my sister Stephanie for the first time ever!

I had been given up for adoption when I was born; my mom and dad adopted me when I was about six weeks old. I had always known that both my brother—who had been given up by a different birth mother—and I were adopted and it was never an issue for us. We were both raised with love and affection, and had two parents who would cross oceans for us.

Around 1999, I was successful in locating my birth mother, and I learned that I was actually one of three who were given up for adoption. The other two were girls who shared the same father, whereas I had a different father. My birth mom eventually went on to marry and have another daughter and a couple of sons. She had opened up the path for any of us who chose to look for her, which made it very easy.

I have spoken to all my sisters and my birth mom over the phone and have had the opportunity to meet my birth mom's husband, Geo, once for coffee when he passed through Lethbridge. Beyond that, we tried to stay in contact on Facebook, and through emails, but we had never been able to pull off meeting each other in person. Once I knew I would be going to Ontario, I sent messages to everyone to see if they could somehow make it out our way to Bath. My sister Stephanie was the only one who could make it work.

We planned on having Stephanie and her boyfriend, David, meet us at Bob and Glo's on Monday. That would give me a day or two to settle from the Victor Walk and catch up with Bob and Glo, and another day or two to catch up with my cousin Mike before Stephanie and David came. I felt like I needed to take each event separately, only thinking about the next one once the first had happened. I didn't let myself get excited about seeing Bob and Glo until the walk was over. I didn't let myself get excited about Mike until we had settled at Bob and Glo's, and then I wouldn't let myself get worked up over meeting Stephanie, until after Mike came.

I found I needed to take one thing at a time or I would worry I might just be overwhelmed with too much excitement. I handled that the same way I handle everything in life: I pay attention to only what needs my attention at that moment and then I move on to the next thing, once the first is complete. I find if I try to take too much in at once, I start to zone out.

As things turned out, Steph and David arrived shortly before Mike and his girlfriend Jill arrived. Mom and Bob and Glo had left to take Glo to her radiation treatment, and I was left holding down the fort, waiting for everyone to arrive. I was so glad to have a little bit of time to get to know Steph and to meet David before Mike came; they both fit in very well and I know we will stay connected.

I have always teased Bob and Glo that I was the "favourite niece" and they were "my favourite aunt and uncle," so much so that they often introduce me to others as their favourite niece and we all have a chuckle. The first night we spent together with Steph and David, I wanted to let her know that although she seemed like a nice lady and got along with everyone, she would not be the favourite: that was my job! She laughed and said, "Well you can't be too effing great; Mom gave you up for adoption, too!"

Yes, I could see that we would be getting along just fine. Mike and Jill came and we all got caught up with each other's lives and spent some really good quality time together over the next couple of days.

Thursday morning it was time to head back home after one very full and exciting week. After seven days like that, full of inspiration and hope, I knew my life going forward would never be the same. I knew it was time to do everything I could to make a difference in the lives of others. I had found my voice and lost all my shame; I felt whole.

THE TAKEAWAY LESSON

Sometimes we remain silent out of fear that our family and friends will not support us. I have personally found this to be untrue. We are all worthy of support and acceptance. We remain trapped in silence until we find the courage to take one small step. The step doesn't have to be big, and it doesn't require you to share your story with the world. All that is required is to take a step and to find a safe person to talk to, one who will not judge, just be there to listen. Releasing what is locked inside allows us to begin to heal.

The Spark That Starts The Fire

You might be asking yourself where this journey all began; what prompted my mom and me to hop on a plane to Ottawa and start this journey?

Well, my mom and dad head south to Arizona every year in the winter, and usually come back around the end of March, once the snow melts here at home. This year, starting in January 2013, my mom had mentioned in several of her phone calls from the States, that we had to do something to make a difference to people and we had to start the conversations about child sexual abuse, to raise the awareness of just how often it happens. She was adamant that what I had gone through could not be without a reason, a bigger purpose. In order for her to heal from the guilt of not recognizing what had been happening to me when I was a child, she needed to do something to help other children perhaps from suffering the same fate. I felt the same way: we needed to help others recognize the signs and we needed to encourage victims to speak up.

My mom mentioned a fundraiser she had attended while she was in Arizona, at which the proceeds went toward helping children in need; she thought we should investigate that avenue. I wholeheartedly agreed with her, although I did not have any idea of what was available, or who could help us find out.

Mom and Dad came home in March as they usually do, only this time my mom had a fire in her belly and was hell-bent on getting something going. She went onto the internet to explore (which was a pretty big deal for her, since she hates the computer unless she is playing games), and she came across Theo Fleury's website. Theo said he would be walking from Toronto to the steps of Parliament Hill in Ottawa with a petition and his goal was to lengthen jail terms for pedophiles and increase the awareness of child sexual abuse. The walk was what he called the Victor Movement. He urged people to sign the petition and to either join him in Ottawa, or take part in the walk that was happening in their own cities.

Needless to say, Mom called me right away. She told me to get onto Theo's website (www.theofleury14.com), and to sign the petition. So I checked it out. Now I had heard about this Theo guy and his book *Playing With Fire* , but I had never thought that what he had to say would resonate with me so strongly. Maybe it was that I just wasn't ready to hear it before then. At any rate, I looked up the petition and read all I could about this Victor Movement. Immediately, I knew I had to be part of it. I called my mom and told her I had signed the petition and also had sent the link to everyone I knew. I had reached the end of my solo suffering and could feel it in the deepest part of my soul. I knew I had to be on the steps of Parliament Hill with him.

"Looks like we are going to Ottawa, Mom," I said with conviction.

She was thrilled!

The Victor Movement was also raising funds for organizations that help victims of child sexual abuse; the one that stood out the most to me was a group called "Little Warriors," which focuses on the education and prevention of child sexual abuse. I contacted Little Warriors to get receipt books for donations and to talk to them about what they needed and how I could help them. I was immediately impressed with how personable the lady on the phone was. We talked about their vision, their education program, and about a dream they had for building a treatment facility for children that would be called "Be Brave Ranch."

This organization was also familiar to me, much the same way that Theo Fleury was, in that I had heard about them, looked at their website (www.bebraveranch.littlewarriors.ca), and decided it was not for me at the time. Now, all of a sudden, there I was again with both of them on my radar and they were both "speaking" very loudly to the core of my being.

I remember saying over and over that I wasn't sure why this was pulling at me so strongly, but I did know that whatever the reason was, it just didn't matter. What mattered was that I felt like maybe I could make a difference to a child somewhere, or to an adult, who like myself, had suffered alone in silence for too many years.

In my phone conversation with Little Warriors, they mentioned a young girl who lived in a town close to me. They told me how, in 2012, this girl had raised $9,100 by getting people to sponsor light bulbs on a big tree in her hometown of Coaldale, Alberta. Each light represented a victim and the idea was to "shed light" on child sexual abuse. The money that was raised through her event was donated to Little Warriors to help them build the Be Brave Ranch.

At that time, millions of dollars were needed and they were a very long way from raising the money that could help to make this dream a reality. The Alberta Government had not approved any funding for this facility; however, it was expected that the approval for funding would eventually appear. In the meantime, Little Warriors had no intention of sitting on their laurels waiting for this to magically happen. They were busy rallying the public for support. This facility would be the first treatment centre of its kind in North America, and very long overdue. Although we have resources for the offenders in this country, we had yet to provide for the victims. So, there I was, armed with a bit of information and a whole bunch of enthusiasm, along with two plane tickets to Ottawa to join Theo on Parliament Hill.

My dad, who has always supported me, asked why I felt I had to go all the way to Ottawa. Wasn't there something I could do in Lethbridge? I answered the only way I knew how. "What if everyone said, 'Why do you have to go all that way?' What if, after everything that was being done to change the face of how we deal with child sexual abuse, everyone just brushed it off and let someone else deal with it? What if this helps even just one child feel less alone? What reason is there for everything that I went through, if not to make things better? What if Theo ended up on the steps of Parliament alone?"

We as victims have faced such incredible adversity head on and often all by ourselves. It is time for us to change that, time for us to hold our heads high and walk together. Thanks to the Victor Movement, many of us no longer refer to ourselves as victims; we are now Victors and we no longer walk alone; we "Walk With Thousands," just as in the title of the song that Theo and his band The Death Valley Rebels perform.

Shortly after Mom and I bought our tickets, I began to spread the word about the Victor Movement and the petition as best I could. I shared links on Facebook whenever I saw them, and for the first time ever, I publicly said I had been abused. I was so sad that nobody wanted to share my posts or comment on them, and very few people even indicated they had seen them.

I kept thinking about the statistics and how if one in three girls and one in five boys are affected, how could we continue to feel awkward about this topic? Is it possible that the ones who are victims wouldn't comment because they don't want anyone to know they have been abused? For sure, that is a very real possibility. The other reason, like it or not, is that it made people uncomfortable. Unless somebody is personally affected, or loves someone who has been affected, they just do not see themselves supporting this conversation publicly. The truth of the matter is that most people do love someone who is affected, and it would be fair to say that most of us are not even aware of it, because the abused person has not yet told anyone.

I had someone say to me once they thought it would be impossible to hide something like that and that there was no way a parent wouldn't know if their child had been abused. That is what my parents would have said up until when I came forward at the age of twenty-four, when I was pregnant with my son. My parents tortured themselves for the next twenty years, wondering how they could not have seen what was happening; how could they not have known?

The reason for that was quite simple: I did not want them to know.

Period.

Shortly after Mom and I made the decision to join Theo in Ottawa, a high-risk child sex offender was released from prison and a warning was released to the public that he would be living in the city where I lived, Lethbridge. I shared the warning post from our local police department on Facebook and, as usual, barely anyone shared or commented. The exception was my husband Lou, who shared the post and commented that I would be going to Ottawa to join Theo Fleury and how proud he was of me, and all that I was trying to do.

Soon after that, I received a message on Facebook from a lady who didn't know me or my husband, but had seen Lou's post on Facebook and had tracked me down to let me know that I was not alone, and that she was happy to hear I would be going. She asked me if I would be interested in meeting her and her daughter for coffee, since it was always nice to meet someone else who was passionate about the same thing.

Well, wouldn't you know it? The lady who called was Heather Lee and her daughter was Alison Lee, the teenager from Coaldale who had held the "Shed Light" fundraiser. Wow, I must admit I was pretty impressed with this young lady. I was also amazed that just the previous week I had been talking on the phone with Little Warriors and now, through the magic of Facebook, we had met and were wasting no time at all planning our future endeavours together.

At the time we met, Alison was also hoping to be able to go to Ottawa to participate in the Victor Walk with Theo. It didn't look like there would be a way this family of five was going to be able to make that happen for her, short of a miracle that is.

We kept in touch and met up for another coffee, a couple of weeks later. The more I spoke to Alison, the more I wished we could find a way to get her to Ottawa. I asked her mom if she would allow Alison to go if I found a way to make it happen. I assured her I would take good care of Alison and that my mom and I wouldn't mind having her stay with us in the event that we somehow could get her on a plane with us. Heather agreed to let her go, so I went home and put out a post on—you guessed it—Facebook. I explained the situation and just asked if anyone out there had Air Miles they wanted to share with us to help her get to Ottawa.

I got a message the very next day from a kind woman who had been a good friend of mine in high school. She was willing to donate her Air Miles, as well as pay the taxes that went along with the ticket. I could barely believe it! Along with her offer to help was an extremely touching message of thanks to me for having the courage to speak up and trying to raise awareness. She spoke of being a victim herself and how much it meant to her that I had found my voice.

In all the years that had passed since she and I had been teenagers, I had forgotten that she too was a victim and, I am ashamed to say, I was so wrapped up in myself at the time that I had forgotten her story, the one that took so much courage for her to share with me. I'm not sure what moved me more: the fact that she had so generously offered assistance to Alison, or that she was so damn encouraging and thankful for what I had done.

For the first time in my life, I had a glimmer of hope that someone would benefit from me finding my voice.

The very next day, I had another message from an associate offering to donate Air Miles. I can tell you I was beyond thrilled with the generosity being shown. When I let the second donor know that Alison's ticket had been taken care of already, she offered to contribute her Air Miles for Heather, Alison's mom. And now we have a full-blown, mother-daughter, powerhouse road trip. It would be the first of many.

In the days that led up to Ottawa, I continued to receive messages of encouragement and thanks, as well as numerous donations to help Little Warriors. I was still somewhat discouraged with the lack of public support, but the private messages were more than enough to let me know that there were many survivors out there, all waiting to find their voices.

The weeks leading up to the Victor Walk in Ottawa went by quickly. We filled our time helping Torre, the Lethbridge Victor Walk Coordinator, get the word out about the walk that would be taking place in Lethbridge while we were in Ottawa.

My head was swimming with a mixture of excitement and fear. I was so worried that we would go all that distance and end up alone with Theo on the steps of Parliament. I prayed there would be others beside us, all willing to find the courage to stand up and be heard. I worried for Theo that, after all he was trying to do, the world wouldn't be ready to hear what so desperately needed to be said. I can remember thinking that if that ended up being the case, we would just go back again and again and again, until we had support. It was time for change, and it was long overdue for us to stand united as Victors and shed some light on this topic.

The night before we left for Ottawa, the four of us, along with my daughter Ali and Torre, the Lethbridge Victor Walk Coordinator, all went and got henna tattoos put directly on our forearms of the Victor Walk mascot who is affectionately referred to as Victor, and just happens to be a cool frog. United we stand!

Finally, the day to leave came. My mom and I flew separately from Alison and Heather, because of the seat availability for the Air Miles flights. Alison and Heather arrived a few hours before us and spent their time at the Ottawa International Airport making posters for our walk while waiting for us to land. Alison had made signs that said things like, "I Can't Be Broken, Not Anymore!" and "I Am Brave."

When Mom and I finally arrived at the terminal and made our way down the escalator, there Alison and Heather were: bright orange Victor shirts on and posters in hand! There was a lady talking on her cell phone standing not too far away from them. She came over after her call ended and told us she was so excited to see us there for the walk, and that she had been talking to Theo when we arrived. She'd let him know we were there for the walk and told us she was relieved to see the support. She introduced herself as Celina; we have kept in touch since via Twitter posts.

We were so worried that we wouldn't know where to go for the Victor Walk that was to take place the next morning and really wanted to know how long it would take us to walk from our hotel over to the steps of Parliament, so off we went in preparation! Everyone donned their Victor shirts and we hoped people would see us, and that the excitement would build.

It was very muggy in Ottawa and there was a light misting of rain that night. Still, we walked on and made our way to our destination, taking pictures the whole way. We reached the main entrance to the Parliament Building and there was an RCMP officer parked on the roadway in front. He came over and talked with us for a while. He supported what we were there for and asked for photos of us with him. The humidity and misting rain didn't help with the quality of the photos, but we got them, frizzy hair and all!

We made our way back to the hotel, eventually. Heather and I stayed outside to have a smoke before we went in, and Mom and Alison went up to the room.

Shortly after they had left us to go up, a man came out and remarked about us being there for the walk too. He was by himself and had just seen two other girls in the elevator wearing Victor shirts. We explained that we were all together and continued to chat with him for at least an hour. This man's name is Brian. He was very friendly and the conversation came easily. He had never publicly spoken about the abuse he suffered as a child. In fact, his wife was more than a little uncomfortable with him even attending the walk. Brian told us she had asked about what to tell their friends if they asked where he was going. Brian told her to tell them the truth.

He also talked about how he had met Theo's team while they were walking in a town along the route to Ottawa. Brian walked alongside them and shared his story with another man. Brian poured his heart out, probably for the first time ever. At one point, Brian said that he turned to the left and there was a big video camera in his face, which caught him by surprise. The cameraman told him that he was filming a documentary and asked Brian for permission to use the footage for the film. Brian told us that before that very moment he would have told the guy, "No effing way!" but for some reason he was tired of being ashamed and tired of hiding, so he said, "Absolutely!"

We made arrangements to meet up the next day and let Brian know that he was more than welcome to join us. Heather had made arrangements for us to meet up with Alex Vorobej for breakfast in the morning before we headed out. Alex is part of Voice Found, which—much like Little Warriors—provides awareness and education about child sexual abuse to individuals and organizations.

Meeting with Alex was a pretty big eye opener for me. Prior to speaking with him, I would have never considered that I—along with other victims of child sexual abuse—could be suffering from varying levels of post-traumatic stress disorder. My whole life, I had felt plagued by periods of time when I would just "space out" and not be there mentally. I can remember, on several occasions, my first husband leaving for work at 7:30 a.m. in the morning, and when I snapped back to reality, it would be 3 p.m. in the afternoon. It felt like minutes had passed, but actually the whole day had gone and I couldn't even begin to tell you what I had really been thinking about all that time. I had been sitting at the kitchen table for hours accomplishing nothing and so would then have to race around like a mad woman trying to tidy dishes and make beds before my husband came home.

I didn't fully understand all the ways that trauma had affected me. It never occurred to me at all that I would continue to feel the aftereffects of my abuse long into adulthood. I had always been pretty hard on myself for what I perceived to be my shortcomings.

When my son was just a little guy, he would wipe out on his bike; I mean really wipe out. As fast as he fell, he would jump back up and announce, "I'm okay, I'm okay." I knew he wasn't really, but for some reason he did not want the attention that "not being okay" would get him.

I look back at my childhood and how I handled my abuse, and I can really see the similarities. I managed to paste a smile on my face and made sure that it would stay there always. If I dared to let my troubles show, "they" would know; everyone would see all my secrets. I was really good at faking it. Everyone thought I was just a happy-go-lucky kid with a big soft heart. I never allowed myself to cry over what was happening to me at the hands of my grandfather. I didn't realize it at the time, but now I know that if I had let myself cry, I might not have been able to stop. I adopted that stiff-upper-lip mentality when I was four and kept it in play for the remainder of my life.

No matter what the situation, I just plowed through, putting one foot in front of the other with a smile on my face. That type of coping took an incredible amount of focus and energy to pull off in the wake of the horrors I endured. While I appeared to be in control, all anyone really had to do to see that I wasn't in control would have been to look at my surroundings: my inability to keep my room clean; trouble with memory in school; binders that, after the first two weeks of school, looked like a bunch of papers stuffed into the binder cover without rhyme or reason.

I could pass something dropped on the floor and I would see it, but not have a message in my brain that said to pick it up. I would pass that paper for days until the level of chaos in my life had settled down. Then all of a sudden, I would look at it and say, "Well, that is silly; let's just pick that up."

I can tell what my stress level is as an adult, just by looking at my car and my purse. When the stress level gets too high, I check out mentally, only letting things that absolutely need to be done register the trigger for action in my brain. The difference now is I can catch myself doing it and force myself to act.

My husband Lou is an obsessive, clean freak and extremely organized, so you can imagine the patience he has had to have to live with me. At least now, I am starting to see there are very good reasons for some of the things I do and that no matter how much I try to jump up and say, "I'm okay, I'm okay," I can acknowledge that childhood abuse affected me in more ways than I care to admit.

THE TAKEAWAY LESSON

People respond differently to different challenges. It is okay to admit that you are not perfect; in fact none of us is. When you begin to understand yourself and why you do the things you do, opportunities for self-growth will be apparent to you. You can't fix what you don't know, and understanding yourself is a great opportunity to make new choices the next time a challenge presents itself.

Chapter Four

Out With The Old; In With The New

Attending the Victor Walk was a game changer for me. We all returned home and I looked forward to jumping right in and getting started with raising awareness to childhood sexual abuse. What I didn't count on was the emotional crash that happened in the next few weeks following our return home from the walk.

We had been flyin' high, all pumped up, and ready to go throughout all the weeks leading up to the walk and also at the walk itself. Somehow, I thought it would be so easy to bring that enthusiasm back with me, that everyone would want to hear about all that I had experienced, a magical light bulb would click on, and people would realize that we as a society have dropped the ball and our children need help.

That was when the reality check came and smacked me right in the face. It wasn't that people were opposed to hearing about the walk at all; in fact they were, generally speaking, very supportive of the stories I told. I had colleagues who had been watching my Facebook posts and offered me words of encouragement. Some even sent me private messages telling me that they too had been affected. But soon enough, I began to be "that girl" who posts every little thing she sees around the topic of child sexual abuse.

Even though I was doing it with the best of intentions, it would become predictable, and people would stop reading the posts. The hard part for me was there wasn't anything really going on in particular that could be used as a stepping stone to have the conversations that would make people more aware. This is one of those topics that people just tend to feel awkward talking about. I understood how they felt, after all it had taken me forty years to even be able to talk about it myself, and to finally and totally remove the feelings of shame that I had carried. How could I expect them to just be like, "Oh I get it. Yes, let's do something together about this!"

Every ounce of my energy in the weeks leading up to the Victor Walk was devoted entirely to that event. Coming home afterward, it was pretty hard to realize that it was just that, an event, a moment in time that was shared with other people who had found their voices. It's not that there was anything wrong with that, but coming back to life and work as it had been before the walk left me feeling like something was missing. I had tasted what it felt like to be totally driven by passion and determination, and I knew that anything I would do from that moment on would pale in comparison unless it was something that would help others also let go of their shame.

What I had failed to realize was that there were many more people out there, just like me, who had also finally been able to remove their shame. Small conversations were starting where previously there had been silence and the Victor Movement was gaining momentum. After having carried our shame for so many years and after feeling the isolation of thinking that we were all alone, we finally had been set free and I don't think that life for any of us will ever be the same.

When you reach a point where you are shown the light and are able to feel it glowing on your face and warming you to the core of your being, the last thing you want to do is to slip back into the darkness that is isolation.

The months after the Victor Walk would prove to be my biggest test. I was forced to learn patience and also to take an inventory of my life to know where I wanted to go and what I wanted it to look like.

This frog was not prepared to stand still; in order to be true to myself I would have to hop forward, even if the hops were small.

At that time, I was the secretary for a branch of the Rotary Club in Lethbridge. I found that even attending Rotary, which I had previously loved, had become a mundane task. I sat and listened as we tried to work out the upcoming year's budget. This was driving me nuts! We were giving money to various international humanitarian projects and here at home in Lethbridge our chosen upcoming local project was to renovate one of the parks in Lethbridge.

I kept thinking, "Man, if the Little Warriors had that money, it would go a really long way toward helping the victims of child sexual abuse."

Everything the club did ended up bouncing back in my head as a distraction to what I really wanted to be doing. Don't get me wrong, our Rotary Club was doing some wonderful things and always tried its best to help where it could. The problem for me was I didn't want to spend the time I was spending at weekly meetings, at other club events, and working on my secretarial duties. I felt like my thoughts were constantly about how to help other child sexual abuse victims; how to get the word out there; how to change our justice system; they were definitely not focused on writing minutes for meetings or selling houses in my career as a full-time real estate agent. There was a war going on inside my mind, a constant pull between what I had to do and what I really wanted to do.

At first, the things that I had to do won the battle. I felt like I wasn't anyone special; I didn't have any special connections or affiliations that would give me credibility to do anything other than what I did to earn my living as a Realtor™ .

As time went on, I realized that everyone who was doing something about the things that I could only dream of doing had all started out being just like me. The only difference was that they acted on their dreams instead of just dreaming them. Sure Theo had his hockey career to give him leverage; but where he is making the biggest impact on society isn't through playing hockey. He hasn't gone to school to learn how to write books and speak publicly; nor has he taken courses on how to motivate and inspire people. All that Theo has done has been a result of his own life experiences and the lessons that he has learned along the way. He has combined those with his passion to help others. Outside his incredible hockey career, he is just like you and me: he has his own fears and insecurities, and feels emotions like sadness and anger and love just like everybody else.

Glori Meldrum, the founder of Little Warriors, has also done incredible things. She is a successful entrepreneur, but that will not be her legacy. Her legacy will be left simply because she refused to sit back and wait for someone else to stand up and help our children who are suffering.

I had grown so used to looking to everyone else for approval of everything I did that I ended up living the life they saw me living. I have two teenage children as well as two stepchildren, and I have spent an incredible amount of time coaching them to find their passion and pursue it; to dream big and then go after the dream. I wanted them to live their lives the way they wanted to live them. I encouraged them to go out and make this world a better place in whatever way they could.

Lou and I have had many conversations since that incredible week in Ottawa and often he started out by showing concern over the lack of attention I was giving to our business and the fact that all of my energy was being put toward raising awareness for child sexual abuse.

He often would say, "What you're doing is important and it is good that you want to help others, but don't forget you are a real estate agent and that's what puts food on our table."

He wasn't being mean, but he just didn't understand the passion that was driving me. How did I expect him to understand my passion when we had spoken so little about what I felt as a result of what I had gone through as a child? After all, I had gone to great lengths to paste on my smile and make sure that everyone thought I was okay, not affected at all by my childhood. Now, here I was, trying to align my actions with my passion, and I was feeling frustrated with what I perceived to be a lack of support. The funny thing about life is that when you let yourself be pulled and pushed along in accordance with someone else's dream, you lose sight of your own dream, or worse yet, fail to dream at all. For me, this directly affected my life; it also affects the lives of others, and I longed for a chance to help everyone I could to understand we need to be in this together. I began to wonder if just maybe I had all the experience in helping others that I needed. I am an expert because I lived it, and you just can't learn that from a textbook.

I wanted to take the prevention and awareness course that Little Warriors puts on called "Stewards of Children"; I was looking forward to that. It was my intention to work toward being able to facilitate the "Stewards of Children" program; attending the course was the first step.

Alison Lee had gone to Edmonton for a photo shoot with Little Warriors a few weeks before the Victor Walk and there was talk about a big ad campaign that would feature those photos. We hoped the release of that ad campaign would be coming soon, but it hadn't happened yet. I felt like a junkie waiting for another "fix"; I needed to feel the positive energy coursing through my veins again, the way it had at the Victor Walk.

Now, after the Victor Walk, I really struggled with the purpose of it all. Did people really need to get a blow-by-blow description of what I had lived through in order to understand it? I had never in my life played the victim role and I sure wasn't about to start using the poor-me card now. I decided to edit what I had written and change its direction over and over and over. At this stage, I was beginning to understand that we all have different roles to play with regard to elevating the conversation, changing our judicial system, as well as encouraging others to speak up. I had been caught in the trap just like a fly to flypaper, trying to solve all the world's problems and getting nothing done.

I kept writing a little here and a little there, but floundered with the purpose, so I was never really able to sink my teeth into it. I had spent an incredible amount of time deliberating, in my mind, the different options that might help me to reach people. I wished I had the ability to see the future and to know without a doubt what it was that I needed to do. Was it that I needed to publish a book? Should I be looking into going back to school to educate myself to be a counsellor or a therapist? I just didn't know. I was feeling stuck.

I was also feeling very thankful that at least I enjoy what I do for a living. I love being able to help people find the house that is just right for them, to watch their faces as they walk through the door of a home that really speaks to them, and then to be able to make sense of all the legalities and paperwork for them. I love that Lou and I can do that together and that we are able to help each other out when needed.

What I couldn't shake was the feeling that just maybe my passion and my career are not one and the same. I told myself it is rare for people to be able to earn a living doing what they are absolutely passionate about. That is why people have hobbies and interests outside work. I don't think I would have felt so conflicted if I didn't like my job so much. It offers me security, a roof over my head, the chance to meet some really great people, and to help them out as well. It simply was not practical for me to be off in Lalaland dreaming about following my passion, nor was it responsible. I needed to focus on doing what I had to do today, so I could do what I wanted to do tomorrow; that is the reality of life.

A few months prior to the Victor Walk, I had attended a district conference for Rotarians. The agenda included a competition with presentations on the last day from a group of youth who attended an area conference for teens who had been identified as leaders among their peers. The competition was based on the following question, "What is the biggest challenge facing youth today and what is your solution to overcome it?"

On Sunday morning, the last item on the agenda was to listen to the various presentations given by these teens. I was told later that the group of teens got together and wrote down a number of challenges and then each person was able to pick which group they personally identified with the most and to join that team to determine a solution. Every presentation was outstanding and each of them had been well thought out and delivered in exactly the way you would expect youth leaders to present something like this. The two presentations that stood out the most to everyone in the group of three hundred Rotarians who were in the audience were the ones that talked about abuse.

While we Rotarians talked about our international projects and discussed different ways to help women and children and entire villages abroad, these teens were taking care of business right here at home, and opening our eyes to the shortcomings of our systems and the children who fall through the cracks as a result.

The audience sat and listened in awe as these insightful teens brought home the need for action right here at home. Each group brought forward stories of how abuse had touched them. One young lady stood in front of this group of three hundred adults and spoke about her childhood and how abuse led her to be removed from her home and put into foster care. She sobbed throughout her story and had the audience crying right along with her. At the end of her story, she thanked us for the opportunity to share it and told us she had never told anyone about this before.

She finished talking and the room exploded in thundering applause and a standing ovation. Story after story unfolded, our eyes were opened more and more as the stories evolved. The group that won the competition had picked abuse as their topic and some of them described how they had experienced abuse and watched as friends suffered through it without the help of the adults in their lives.

They spoke about the lack of resources available to teens who are in need and why kids in trouble do not seek out help through the channels that are available. They then talked of how abused children turn to various other means of coping with their situation. Some turn to drugs and alcohol, some to cutting themselves, some run away only to be labelled as problem children, and some just stuff all their emotions as far down as they can in order to remain as normal looking as possible; others attempt suicide. They talked about the lack of trust toward adults and counsellors and the legal system. They watched how those who do come forward are either not believed, or if they are believed, are forced to stay with the abuser. Some watched abusers get a slap on the wrist and return to the home to carry on worse than before.

The next problem was what brought it all home to me.

Children will not come forward if the rest of their life is normal. Why would they risk that bit of normal in their lives only to have their worlds turn upside down? They told us that the abusers are often family members who are loved by the victims and therefore protected. What results from that is the child carries a tremendous amount of guilt and a certain ownership over what happens to them.

What they felt was needed was a place where teens can go to feel safe after school and on weekends, a place where they can build friendships and trust with those around them, get help with homework, play instruments or games or music, a place run by teens or young adults where secrets are safe, and they can confide in others if they choose to, or at the very least know that they are not alone, and can build self-confidence and self-esteem. They spoke of the trickle effect that abuse has on our social systems; how the cycle of being a victim carries on until the victim gains control and feels like they are not to blame, and are strong enough and worthy enough to live a life that doesn't include abuse in one form or another.

What these teens were saying was not anything that I did not know firsthand already. What I wasn't prepared for was the overwhelming response that the audience gave them. It was clear that people were shocked by the topic and wanted to do everything that they could to help.

As soon as the presentations were complete, Rotarians were standing up to offer support both financially and otherwise. I slipped over to one group and gave them my card and let them know that they were onto something so huge that people everywhere needed to hear what they had to say. They all sat stunned, some crying, and overwhelmed with the response from their audience. One girl said that when they started this, they were just thinking of the competition and now they realized that they really could make a difference. They realized that what they do can change people's lives forever. They suddenly were forced to accept responsibility for following through on what they could do to help.

Up until I had attended that conference, I felt compelled to put my story on paper. I wanted to make a difference in the lives of other people who had also gone through tough times. I didn't want to be a victim. I want to be a survivor who is thriving and using my adversities to make positive changes in the lives of those around me. I had a very hard time putting my story on paper, often writing a line or two every few months, and then finding the process too painful to continue. It seemed pointless to endure that much pain while recounting every detail of my abuse just to possibly help the one or two people who might care to read my book. I just didn't think anyone would care to read my story without my having any purpose for telling it.

It was at that conference, surrounded by amazing individuals from all walks of life, that I realized I didn't need to tell all the details of the abuse. I needed to help all the "lost children" and to give them a voice. The people who hear their stories will be moved to help make the changes they can, in their own unique ways, and the stories will spread along with a new awareness of where we are falling short and the effect that has on our younger generations. I brought back those thoughts and embraced the fire that had started in my belly.

As a relatively new Rotarian, I had been scheduled to do a vocational talk at our club during the next meeting following the conference. I had been struggling with what to talk about. I could talk about earning my living as a Realtor™ and I could also discuss my previous work history that led up to that point. I could also discuss such points as how many children I had and where I grew up and went to school. What I struggled with was the fact that every time I thought of the word "vocation," I thought of the word "calling." I didn't feel that any of these talks would be a reflection of who I am or how I came to be this person.

After leaving that conference, it became clear to me that I needed to echo my experience when listening to the youth competition, and share with my club how and why that related to my life and what I felt "called" to do as a result. All my fear of what to say had diminished. I wasn't talking about anything other than my experiences and how they reflected what the youth at the Rotary conference had said.

My club responded to my story with such enthusiasm and respect that I knew I was on the right track. The more victims there are who come forward, the more awareness there will be around the topic and, hopefully, that will start a chain reaction of other people coming forward as well.

When I was growing up, abuse had no place at meal-table discussions or in discussion among peers. The media was not obsessed with the topic and very little was ever heard about what went on.

I can remember as a teenager, the topic of rape being discussed in court cases, and how the general consensus was to not condone rape, but also to question the actions of the victims and how they carried themselves or dressed, and what role that played in each case. I know that too many women were left to defend themselves and prove that they had not brought such things onto themselves.

As a teenager, I had a friend confide in me that her father had sexually abused her, and when she came forward, her mother and brothers disowned her and kicked her out of the house for "having an affair" with her father. She was put into foster care and was devastated at the lack of support she had received from everyone involved. At that time, those situations alone left me with enough self-doubt to ensure that I too kept quiet and endured my abuse in silence.

But times have changed since then and there is now a greater awareness of abuse of all types; our social systems have responded with counsellors for victims and child welfare organizations, which are both now overbooked. The problem has gone from being buried to being wide open and exposed. The question is whether we are helping those who need it in a way that will encourage others to also seek help. Or are too many victims falling through the cracks and becoming victims of the very services that are in place to help them?

When I was a teenager, I longed for the love and acceptance that comes with being in a relationship. I wanted nothing more than for someone to want to spend the rest of his life with me. I was full of the usual self-doubt that plagues all teens; the only difference was that I had spent the majority of my life in silence about what had happened to me. I felt very much alone and I bore a tremendous amount of guilt for that as well. Holding in my story had the effect of wreaking havoc on my self-esteem and my confidence level. That led to my making poor or inappropriate choices in my relationships and having a skewed vision of what "normal" is. It was pretty much inevitable that I would run into problems along the way.

Now I can see the bigger picture. Thanks to the Victor Walk, I hope to be able to help others come forward so that situations like the ones described by the RYLA students and by other victims can somehow have different, more positive outcomes.

In light of my newfound passion of raising awareness and being an advocate for victims of child sexual abuse, I made the decision to not renew my membership in Rotary and instead to focus my attention toward the areas where my passion lies. It was a tough decision, but one I felt I needed to make. I had my fingers in too many pots and there are only so many hours in a day. It was necessary for me to pull back in order to be able to move forward in the direction I want to go.

The summer months flew by and, while I had been kept very busy with realty work, I still managed to find time to write and also attend the prevention and response program for adults called "Stewards of Children." Little Warriors presents it using content developed by an organization called "Darkness To Light." The program was held on a Saturday and was only about three-and-a-half-hours long. It provided me with a greater understanding of the roles that we as adults have in helping to protect our children. It also provided information about what to do if a child discloses their abuse.

When I consider the impact that each of us as adults can have in changing the way we protect our children, I am baffled by the fact that this program isn't made mandatory in our schools and every other place where children might be involved. It is my dream that one day the government will mandate this program for all adults in schools, youth groups, sports teams, children's camps, and every place where adults interact with children.

With the summer months behind and autumn fast approaching, I found myself doing whatever I could in order to help raise awareness for Little Warriors' goal of building the Be Brave Ranch. Even though what I had been doing was limited to sharing Facebook posts that Little Warriors and its founder Glori Meldrum put out, I began to dream of holding a fundraiser in Lethbridge. I had nothing specific put together except for a desire to help build a place where our children who have been affected by the trauma of sexual abuse can heal.

Alison Lee finally had a date set for when Little Warriors' new ad campaign would be launched; this was the launch for the photo shoot that she had taken part in back in May before the Victor Walk. Alison was pretty excited about the campaign and couldn't wait for it to be launched. I was also wanting to show my support, so I emailed Glori and asked if she thought it would be all right if I attended along with my mom, Alison, and her mom Heather. In her welcoming nature, Glori said that she would be thrilled if we tagged along. I decided to put my dreams of having a big fundraiser on hold for a while, since an event of that magnitude requires plenty of planning and that would take time, something I had very little of.

For now, I felt I needed to take my time and see where things would take me. I kept reminding myself that I would have to be satisfied with doing what I could right now and trust that in the future things would have a way of working themselves out.

THE TAKEAWAY LESSON

Growth is a process. Be patient with yourself and those around you. Change can be scary, even when it is a positive change. Start by visualizing the big picture and then take small steps toward your goal.

Chapter Five

Building Support for the Be Brave Ranch

On September 15, 2013, I celebrated my forty-fourth birthday with my family. I had been really looking forward to turning forty-four, since my favourite number is four and there just happen to be two of those numbers in that age! I had wanted a Victor the frog tattoo for some time and had asked Theo's people for permission and gotten it months before. I didn't know where I was going to put it, but I wanted to be sure it was somewhere visible so that whenever someone asks me about it, I can let them know what it represents.

Since I hadn't yet made the move to get the tattoo done, Lou paid for the tattoo for my birthday; he booked the appointment for the morning before Mom, Heather, Alison, and I left for Edmonton for the press release for the Little Warriors new ad campaign, "Everyday Albertans."

I decided to put it on my wrist.

I was pleased to tell the tattoo artist the story behind the frog and what it means to me. The poor guy felt as though he was prying when I explained to him the reason behind it all. I felt badly for him and assured him that the whole reason behind having it on my wrist was because I want to have these conversations; they are conversations that people need to start feeling comfortable having and this is just my way of doing my part to raise awareness. I let him know that both my mom and daughter also want the same frog tattoos as a show of support for me, as well as to have them serve as a catalyst for conversations.

My mom is one of those special ladies who just loves to do nice little things that aren't expected. For our trip this time, she made some Welsh cakes and cookies, and even sandwiches for Heather who would not have time to eat before we left town, because she would be just getting off work. This ensured that my mom would be dubbed "Favourite Grandma Bev"!

My mom and I have a very special relationship and relish every chance we get to "talk smack" to each other or tease each other in some way. I know there have been times that we are bantering back and forth, when the people around us give us looks of total shock. For us, the joy in razzing each other comes from the fact that absolutely all of what we say is bullshit and we actually adore each other's company immensely and have, contrary to what it would look like, an incredible amount of respect and love for each other. The bantering usually increases when we have an audience and we really kick it into high gear, trying to get people to take one side over the other. Mom usually gets all the votes since it is so damn hard to beat an angel!

My mom loves to shop, in fact the woman can smell a sale from miles away; it's a gift, and she rarely pays full price for anything. When we drove to the Be Brave Ranch right past Cross Iron Mills Shopping Centre, she kicked up a fuss and told us that maybe the next day on the way back to Calgary from Edmonton, we should stop in there and shop…just a little. We all knew there would be no way of that happening on this trip, since the press release in Edmonton was scheduled for first thing in the morning and then we would have to hustle to Calgary for another press release in the afternoon.

We told Mom that if she behaved, we would try to sneak in for a quick shopping fix. Total lie, I know, but sometimes it's fun to mess with her. It was pretty late by the time we got settled into our hotel room, but not too late to perform my famous steam roller move on Mom, where I roll from one side of the bed right over her and onto the other side of the bed. It got a laugh when I did it in Ottawa and so I figured, what the heck, let's go for an encore. Sure enough the result was hysterical laughter followed by snorts and giggles that kept us awake far later than we should have been.

I don't know if you've ever experienced just how difficult it is to fall asleep in a room full of women. First, everybody has to "shut the hell up," and then the giggles start, which then work their way into full-blown hysterical laughing, and eventually get followed by snorts and sighs. And then the laughing starts up all over again, and nobody even has a clue what the hell was so funny that had started it all. Eventually the shenanigans stopped and I was left with nothing but the quiet sounds of sleeping and the thoughts that were bouncing through my head.

I was pretty excited about the chance to meet Glori Meldrum—the founder of Little Warriors—in person, and I felt so honoured to actually be able to attend this press release, just to witness it. Glori had known Alison for some time and I felt like I already knew her through all the stories that Alison had told.

At this point I still felt very much like an outsider with my face pressed up against the glass, waiting to be invited inside. Theo Fleury was also expected to be at the release in Calgary and I was looking forward to hearing him speak again too.

Prior to this road trip, Alison had tried to ask the Province of Alberta's Premier Alison Redford why the Government of Alberta had not committed to help fund the Be Brave Ranch yet; the meeting hadn't gone so well. Alison made an emotional video of her account of the meeting and that video went viral on Twitter. The local news stations and even the national ones were after Alison for interviews and the story even hit the *Lethbridge Herald*.

There was quite an uproar about the whole thing and Alison was even accused of being sent by the Little Warriors to call out the Premier which, by the way, couldn't have been further from the truth. Alison had been busting her hump trying to raise money for the ranch and doing what she could to raise awareness. As a young person who had experienced the trauma of abuse first-hand, it was a very personal plea for assistance for herself as well as for other child victims. Alison was fifteen at the time and wanted to see the ranch become a reality so that she could attend it as a victim trying to heal. She knew that if funding didn't come soon, she would be an adult and that window of opportunity would be closed to her.

Anyway, it was during this whirlwind of attention that I asked Alison to help me get a Twitter account. I really had no idea what it was all about, this tweeting, retweeting, favouriting, and what have you. I felt pretty old and a bit embarrassed at my lack of hipness! Alison set me up as twitter.com/kbenis1, and then whenever there was a tweet about funding for the Be Brave Ranch or anything else related to that or to Little Warriors, she would include me in it. I "followed" Glori and Little Warriors and a couple of other people I had met along the journey.

One night while going through the Twitter feed, I received a notification that Theo Fleury was following me and I couldn't believe it. That was probably one of the first real times that I felt like I belonged to part of a bigger community—the community of Victors—and, let me tell you, it felt pretty awesome.

I know I have mentioned it before, but I really do think of Theo as a hero for this cause, and although his sports background and everything else he has done is impressive, it isn't at all what gives him a "famous" status in my books. He is famous to me just like Glori is: these are two people who have gone to great lengths to change the face of childhood sexual abuse and how those of us who have lived through that trauma see ourselves.

I had tweeted a few photos of the Victor Walk on Twitter along with the video that Torre had made for me telling about my story and why I supported the Victor Walk. I couldn't believe it when Theo and Glori shared what I had posted by re-tweeting. I mean, really, now that I look at it, why wouldn't they? But at the time, I had been feeling so insignificant in all of this compared to what they were doing every day. Having them actually take the time to do something small such as retweet or comment or share a post of mine did something amazing inside me: it showed me that I do matter and that I can make a difference and that they were standing side by side with all of us doing what we can together to make a difference.

Spending time with Alison has also helped to take away some of the awe that I felt toward them, since she often mentioned them and the conversations they have had and I guess I just got a little desensitized to it all, though not enough to keep me from being absolutely thrilled about getting to know them.

Alison would often tease on our road trips and at future meetings, that none of us would have ever gotten to know Glori and Theo at all if it weren't for her and we would never be at the press release if it weren't for her. She was kind of right, at least about the timing of it all, but I know for sure that we were all destined to be fighting for this together and that there were just too many perfectly aligned stars on this journey for any of it to be an accident. I just teased Alison back and said, "Nah, I was already going to Ottawa for the Victor Walk when I met you; you were just along for the ride!"

To which she usually replied, "Ya, but I'm cute!" and who the hell can argue with that logic?

Anyhow, back to the press conference! We woke up pretty early, since we weren't really sure how to get to the press release venue and didn't want to chance being late. Heather was a pretty good chauffeur and we arrived on time as planned. We met up at a small park in downtown Edmonton, and Alison wasted no time at all introducing my mom and me to Glori.

Everyone was always talking about how wonderful Glori is and how sweet and pretty and kind and compassionate and, in general, just a wonderful human being. You know what? That is exactly what I saw in her from the moment we met. She gave Mom and me the biggest hugs, thanked us for our support, and told us she was so happy that we could make it. I went from feeling like an outsider to feeling welcome and accepted, and all it took was thirty seconds and a hug.

Mom and I walked down to the corner coffee shop and grabbed a bite to eat and coffees, while Alison went over what was expected of her at the press release. It was all so surreal. What had seemed like a distant dream was all of a sudden right there in front of me. It really did change the way I looked at myself and the ability I have to make a difference.

In that small park, they had set up a podium with a microphone for Glori to address the media and the supporters who were in attendance. It was placed in front of a gazebo in one corner of the park. Displays representing the different ways that Everyday Albertans had pulled together to help raise funds for the Be Brave Ranch filled the rest of the area.

One display of a tree with lights on it represented Alison's "Shed Light" campaign; there was a bike all decked out with Little Warriors' items, representing a poker run that one lady put on; canvas paintings were set out on a table to show how one young girl had painted them and auctioned them off at a fundraising event; and then there was the coolest lemonade stand to show how another young girl had sold lemonade and donated the money to the ranch. There was a big screen showing some samples of the commercials that would air on television and sound bites from the radio commercials. There were others, too, but the whole idea was to show that here were people, Everyday Albertans, who felt that this ranch is important enough for them to try and help get it started without the government's support.

We need that ranch and, come hell or high water, Albertans will build it.

When it came time to talk about Alison's campaign, a huge bus pulled around the corner and there, plastered on the side of it, was our beautiful Alison holding up her light. I looked over at Alison and she was mouthing to her mom, "Look! I'm on the bus!" She barely had time to digest that when it was her turn to talk briefly about what the ranch meant to her and why she felt it was important to get it running.

Glori and the rest of the group pulled off the press release without a hitch; it was very impressive indeed. I tried so hard to get good pictures of Alison's bus and the other displays, but it was pretty hard to do with tears streaming down my face and snot dripping from my nose. I was overtaken by my emotions of gratitude and total appreciation for what was happening. Not only were we helping to build the ranch, we were putting child sexual abuse right out there for everyone to see and hear about. We were very proudly sending a message that the silence over this issue and the shame of it will end here and now, because we aren't playing along with that anymore; we are done!

Just as soon as the last photo op and the last interview were over, Glori apologized to Alison and said, "Sorry, kiddo. We gotta get our butts to Calgary and we have to leave right now."

We agreed to stop in Red Deer for lunch at McDonalds, ran to our vehicles, and we were off! Most of the 155 kilometres to Red Deer, we talked about how great the press release had been, how cool it was to have seen that big bus pull around the corner with Alison plastered all over the side of it, and how great it was to meet Glori. Pretty soon there we were, all sitting together at the restaurant eating lunch. Glori sat down beside me, took one look at my Victor tattoo and flipped. She looked at me and said, "My God, Theo is gonna shit when he sees that!"

She also told me about how it was that her company—GSquared—had designed it for him. Knowing that made it even more special to me. It was a pretty important on-the-fly meeting for Glori and Alison. Among other wonderful things that were discussed, Glori offered Alison a job at the ranch the following summer and Alison, of course, flipped. Now it was time for Alison to help others to be brave and the focus took a shift from her and landed on helping other children. She would be making a real difference in the lives of others and that, my friends, is truly something special.

We made our way to Calgary, and Heather and I whispered to

wake Mom up as we passed the Cross Iron Mills mall. She didn't wake up, so I guess she just wasn't that interested in shopping after all!

We arrived at the country club location for the next shooting of the press release fairly early; in fact, I think we were pretty much the first ones there. Slowly but surely people started to arrive and the press set up for another round of videotaping and interviews. Theo also arrived and spent most of his time talking to people while we waited to start.

I ended up standing beside a lady named Becky and we hit it off pretty well. She was another one of those people whom I have met over the last year and recognized immediately that we were meant to know each other. She was so easy to talk to and I felt as though I could share anything with her. We chatted about next year's Victor Walk and that was when she told me she had been on the walk from Toronto to Ottawa with Theo and they had planned on meeting later on that evening to discuss the plan of action for the next walk. I told her how much I wanted to be a part of the next walk and how I would be thrilled to help out in whatever way I could. I'm sure she thought I was a little nuts, but I couldn't help myself; I just so badly wanted to be on the other side of the glass, instead of with my face pressed up against it, looking in.

Anyhow, my mom was around chatting with us about the whole Victor thing and once she knew that Becky knew Theo, she couldn't resist asking her to take me to him so that he could see my tattoo. I was a little embarrassed and said that no we did not need to go see Theo; if he came up and talked, we could show him then; otherwise, absolutely not; no way were we going to go and show him!

After the interviews and press release were finished, people started slowly leaving; a small handful of us milled around chatting. I looked across a small field to where Theo was. He was taking off his blazer and starting to roll up his sleeve. He walked straight over to me and said, "LET'S SEE IT!" as he held out his forearm with his frog tattoo exposed. It was an "I'll show you mine if you show me yours" stance. Yup. Not gonna lie; that was pretty fricking cool!

This time, we chatted a little bit and I remembered to ask him to sign his book *Playing With Fire* for me. When I handed him the book, he looked up and said, "That's Kelli with an 'i' right?"

He knew my name! Holy crap; he knew my name, and he even knew how to spell it! Wow. I'm sure that Glori had filled him in about the tattoo and told him my name; but still, just the fact that he took the time to come over and remember my name really meant a lot to me. I think for the first time, when he did that, I felt like just maybe we were on the same level; we were just two people determined to change the face of abuse.

After he signed my copy of his book, I held it out at arm's length and he put his forearm against mine and we got a photo of that, which to date is my favourite photo of all time. I have other photos of us together, but the photo of our tattoos with his book symbolize to me that we are working together to help victims become Victors and we are both ignited by the same fire. Together, we will do what we can to help others be free of their shame.

The only drawback of having the two tattoos together was that his was so bitchin'! Mine looked so plain beside his big beautifully shaded masterpiece. I guess when you're the head frog, you get to have the best tatty, and I still love mine. It speaks to me and honours my passion and that is enough.

THE TAKEAWAY LESSON

Be an active participant in your own life. Open yourself up to new experiences and to meeting new people. Watching from the sidelines is a good place to start, but once you are comfortable it is time to get off the bench and jump into the game.

Chapter Six

RYPEN

After Theo left, we stood around and chatted for a short while. Mom and I carried on with our game of "Let's see who can be the meanest to the other" and Glori chose Mom as the sure-fire winner as she munched on one of Mom's cookies. Glori hugged us goodbye with a promise to see us again very shortly, followed by a giggle. She told Mom that she would love to have her help on road trips and she could bake everyone cookies; Glori sweetened the deal by even promising to take her shopping. Glori made me promise to take care of "our Mom" for her and we were off for home. We speculated what the next meeting would be and thought that maybe the Progressive Conservative Government of Alberta would change its decision about funding the ranch; we could only hope.

The evening we returned from the press releases in Edmonton and Calgary, I felt like I was on fire emotionally, like the spark had caught and I was basking in the warmth and glow of it all with no desire to put it out. I was bubbling over with excitement from the events of the past two days. So much had happened that made things real for me. When I looked at the actual events and what had taken place, it wasn't that we had climbed a mountain together or raised a million bucks; that didn't matter at all. We had joined together to support each other and the important dream we were determined to make a reality.

At home, I talked with Lou about all the events of the past two days and how every little thing had gone. Then, in an effort to impress him, I told him about how I even got an autograph from Theo this time. I showed Lou and he said that, although that was pretty cool, he would have been more impressed if I'd actually had Theo autograph his book and written out a message to Lou and not me. Ah. Ya can't win 'em all!

That week had been pretty busy for me—full of things that would pay the emotional and mental health accounts, but not so much the financial bank. I didn't care, and it was easy for me not to, since Lou can always be counted on to worry enough for the two of us.

I enjoyed regrouping the following day, which was a Wednesday, and I looked forward to leaving with my daughter Ali on Thursday to attend RYPEN (Rotary Youth Program of Enrichment), a camp for teens who had been selected by their teachers. As counsellors, we were both pretty excited about sharing the up-coming experience. Ali had attended the camp the previous year as a student and couldn't wait to be a leader this year. She was so excited for me as well, saying this camp would be a game changer and how she knew I knew it was cool, but that my life would never be the same afterward.

I thought maybe that was a bit of an exaggeration, but I did know that it would be a great experience. I had seen the pre-sentations put on for our Rotary Club by the students who had attended the previous year. I'd heard them tell us just how it had made a difference in their lives. It did look pretty darn cool. There would be group activities, team building, and problem solving, as well as wall climbing, a suspension bridge, ziplining, and night hikes—all designed to build trust and confidence.

Ali and I met up with two other leaders and we split up the students from Lethbridge to each of our vehicles. Ali and I took three students in our car, but you would hardly have known that they were even there. Nobody talked except to answer direct questions; they were all plugged into their iPods, trying hard to escape the awkwardness of the drive surrounded by unfamiliar faces.

We drove the students to the Medicine Hat Lodge where every-one signed in and were assigned to one of the five different co-lour groups they would be in for the remainder of the weekend; each of the leaders was assigned a colour group to lead. From there, the students all piled onto buses that we followed out into the Cypress Hills to a place called "The Eagles Nest Ranch."

I had messaged Theo the day before looking for some words of wisdom that I could offer to this group of kids. I'm not sure what I was looking for exactly, but I should have guessed that his response would be, "Don't quit before the miracle." It applies to so many situations in life, particularly when things get tough and we are tempted to just throw our hands in the air and say to hell with it all. Teenage kids have more than their share of situations for which that advice fits so well.

I felt like I needed some sort of reassurance letting me know I was qualified to be there with those kids.

Now, it seems so odd to me that I didn't see at that time just how qualified I really was, and that what I had experienced in my life and how I had gotten through it would provide inspiration to many of those youth. I suppose we all feel confident in certain circles and on our own, but I had just met two of the most inspirational people I have ever had the pleasure of meeting and somehow, for a very short while, I saw all that I had accomplished in life pale in comparison. Those insecure feelings didn't last long though and soon enough I came to understand that I too had the power to motivate and inspire others.

It was at this RYPEN camp that I learned that you don't need to be famous or hugely successful to change someone's outlook on life. You simply need to be there, to listen to him or her, and offer hope for a better tomorrow. When you can get them to believe in themselves, really cool shit starts to happen. Once they see that there is hope, the first thing that they do is offer that message of hope to someone else who needs it, and it is a beautiful thing to watch happen and be a part of.

Sitting in the main lodge at the camp, everyone separated into our colour groups and each of those groups was assigned two leaders. It was plain to see that our work was cut out. Behavioural issues started popping up; students tested the boundaries and made sure that their personal walls were built as high as they could get them; they had no desire to let anyone in—that was far too risky. We then separated into our separate cabins for sleeping. A mixture of each colour group in each of the cabins meant that bedtime started out feeling a little uncomfortable as well.

We started the weekend events with a welcome assembly to go over some of the things that could be expected. Some of us leaders had been asked to talk for a few minutes to the group and offer our insights on a few topics. I was asked to talk about risk taking and the benefits of stepping outside our comfort zones. I wasn't really sure what to say other than that some of the greatest things in life happen to us when we are willing to take risks and without taking those risks, our lives would remain much the same as they have always been—nothing ventured, nothing gained.

I shared how Ali and I were talking one day prior to my speaking to her school during an assembly. I'd had no idea what I was supposed to say and was so worried that I would embarrass Ali by prattling on about nothing. I am like most people who hate to speak publicly; the only exception to that is when I am talking about something I am passionate about. Unfortunately the topic that I was to speak about at her school was something I knew very little about and I felt incredibly out of my comfort zone. While Ali and I were in the car before going into her school assembly, Ali just looked at me and told me to suck it up, put on my "big girl panties" and do it.

It made me laugh out loud, because that is exactly what I would have told her to do, had she been in my situation. She was right though. This was something that I had to do and I should just get over it and do it. I spoke to her school that day and could feel the veins in my neck throbbing the whole time. I actually thought that I might pass out. But in the end I did it; it really wasn't that great a talk; but I did it.

I shared with the RYPEN students my own personal fears of things such as walking into a crowded room by myself, my fear of heights, and also sometimes my fear of meeting new people. Everyone has fears about something and often we are not alone in being afraid. I challenged the students to make this weekend the one when we would try new things together, even if we were afraid. That way we would forever be able to look back at our time at the camp and it would be filled with stories of "I did this while at camp" and not filled with "I wish that I had done that at camp" stories.

I said that some of the greatest things happen when we put ourselves out there to the world and, in the words of one of the most inspirational people I know, I passed on the message, "Don't quit before the miracle." I also challenged them to make sure that they didn't catch me sitting on the sidelines instead of ziplining or walking the suspension bridge; there were a bunch of us who were afraid of heights and likely to opt out without positive encouragement from each other.

Friday morning started with breakfast, which was just as awkward and lacking in conversation as the previous evening's supper had been. A couple of the teens in my group had decided that they could be friends, because they were so similar on the outside. But mostly, there was just awkward silence. We did a few group get-to-know-each-other exercises and soon everyone was remarking about how crazy it was that the other person liked the same music or felt the same about a certain issue. We would discuss things like that and how you just can't judge a book by its cover.

Friday and Saturday, our time was filled mostly with trust-building exercises within our groups. Slowly, the conversations started to warm up. It wasn't until Saturday night, our final night at camp, when things really started to gel.

Each of the groups took turns doing the wall climbing and then taking the suspension bridge over to the zipline platform. Once they completed that, they could enjoy free time until supper. Supper would not be served until the last of the teams made it back to the main lodge after completing the zipline. Nobody would be forced to participate in anything, but they would all be encouraged. There would be no making fun or calling people out; just good solid encouragement was allowed.

Our purple team was the last one to go through the exercises. Every single member of our group, afraid or not, made the climb up the incredibly high ladder to the suspension bridge. We had varying levels of courage displayed at different sections of the challenge by each person. Some would panic when climbing the ladder but then zip across the suspension bridge like it was a cakewalk; others made the suspension bridge, but not the zipline at the end of it. Inevitably, someone would get stuck, frozen in place, unable to move forward. It was then that things really started to get cool. Our group started chanting, "Purple, Purple, Purple," and also yelling words of encouragement to their fellow teammate who was frozen.

The team members on the ground all stepped up and tried to walk their terrified teammate through the fear, shouting. "Just put one foot in front of the other. Watch me over here at the end. Don't look down. You've got this. You're doing so well!"

It literally took a couple of hours before every single person in our purple group made it through. The sun was going down, it was now cold, and we were all very hungry. We felt the pressure of the rest of the groups who had completed the challenge and were waiting for us to return to the main lodge so that they could eat.

None of that mattered to us. We would stand united that day and support one another right through to the end. I was so extremely proud of my purple peeps; we were one and we had at last all bonded together through shared fears, insecurities, and feelings of being a team.

The next challenge would prove to be the biggest, most impactful event of the entire weekend. After dinner, we sent everyone back to their bunks to get their sweats or pyjamas on, and to bring back their pillows. We were about to embark on a sharing exercise that would allow each of them fully to know their teammates, their challenges, and their successes. We had been designated locations around the ranch to allow each group to be able to relax and get comfortable in a space that was private from the other groups—a space of trust if you will.

Each group leader was given a set of questions for each of the team members to answer, on everything from moral situations with no right or wrong answers to who was the person that they most looked up to in life and why. The exercise was designed to last at least an hour and a half, but had no set time limit to it, which meant that if it took until morning for a group to get through it, then so be it.

We had a late start to this final sharing exercise due to the length of time that it took the teams to finish the suspension bridge and zipline challenge, and then get through dinner and into comfy clothes, so the sharing portion started around 9:30 or 10:00 p.m. that night.

For the most part, each group leader would set the stage for the depth of answers that were expected by answering the questions first and then moving to the next person around the circle. Again, nobody would be forced to share anything that they felt uncomfortable sharing, but each would be encouraged to take part.

I found it remarkable to hear the responses. Often there were debates over the answers, but throughout it all there was a profound level of respect given to each person. The final question was, "What is the most difficult thing that you have ever been through and how did you overcome it?"

Again, the leaders shared their stories first to set the tone. I shared my personal story of being sexually abused by my grandfather and how I was working at helping others by writing a book about how I have made it through and am not alone. It took me about fifteen or twenty minutes to tell my story and I could feel compassion from the group over what I had gone through. Once I finished my story, the teens spoke up with words of encouragement and admiration and followed those with big hugs.

Klinton, the other leader, shared the story of his father's death and bravely let himself cry as if it was happening all over again as he told it. The stage had been set and the stories that each teen would tell following ours were filled with equal strife and adversity.

The special part of it all was that everyone in the group poured their hearts out for the whole world to see and they were met with love and acceptance and support. They were shocked that each of us could look so normal and yet had so much pain to get through; they were shocked that without doing that exercise, they would never have known. They spoke about how they had felt when they first arrived at camp: how they were so busy trying to keep from letting anyone connect with them based on what they had assumed others were like just from looking at them. One student remarked that he had friends he'd known since he was in diapers and yet, at that moment, he felt closer to all of us than he had ever felt to any one of those friends.

When these teenagers peeled the outward visible layers away, what they found was that they were all exactly the same. They all felt fear and hate and anger, as well as love and joy and strength. These young people had let down their walls and were finally able to see each other as human beings with hearts filled with dreams and desires just like their own; they were friends, every last one of them.

There was a grand finale talent show planned for after the sharing event, due to begin once the last of the groups ended its sharing session. I can't remember exactly what time it was, but if memory serves me correctly it would have been around 2:30 or 3:00 a.m. in the morning when the last group filed into the main lodge.

Everyone was emotionally spent and physically tired as well.

They were given the choice either to head to bed or to take part in the talent show as planned. As they say in the movies, "The show must go on!" The students who had signed up for the talent show each put on their acts, played instruments, or displayed their artwork for all to see.

My leader partner of team Purple, Klinton, did the very last performance. Klinton is a pretty down-to-earth, quiet, straight shooter whom one would never expect by his outward appearance to be doing anything wild and crazy. He got on stage and performed to the song, "Bust a Move." As the song revved up, so did the audience, and the next thing we knew, students were joining him and dancing on the stage, sort of like a little flash mob. Keep in mind that these people wouldn't even talk to each other two days earlier and now, after going through so much together, they had lost all their inhibitions and were having the time of their lives.

The next morning came time to say goodbye to all our new-found friends. The leaders all lined up along the path to the buses and each student received a hug and words of encouragement from every leader. I was not prepared for how emotional everyone would be. Students begged to be allowed to stay at the camp and, knowing where they came from, it was easy to see why they would ask that.

I was very surprised by the words offered up by each of the students as well. Many told me how I had helped them through this or that, and quite a few told me to "keep my big girl panties on always." The students from Team Purple made me promise to keep in touch and to make sure that I write my book and be sure that they get copies of it. I have never experienced such an emotional farewell in my life. As soon as it was over, Ali and I hugged and cried. We just couldn't help it. I was so proud of Ali that weekend as well, and I could see that she was in fact a true leader and was growing into an absolutely wonderful young woman.

When I spoke to Ali about what she learned most from that camp, she said it was definitely, no matter what, putting yourself out there for meeting new people and trying new things; never allowing yourself to sit on the sidelines of life out of fear of being rejected. She learned that everyone has self-doubts and feels afraid that people will not like them. She realized that by putting yourself out there, you would soon find we are really all in this together. I think that was also one of my big take-away lessons as well, along with a deeper ability to recognize the fronts that people put on in order to protect themselves from getting hurt and feeling rejected.

Sometimes, it is easier for people to dress and act in a way that labels them as "different or weird" than it is to allow themselves to show who they really are inside and risk someone rejecting them for who they are as a person. It is much safer to say that people don't like you because you are Goth or you have your hair dyed blue, than it is to put your real self out there and feel not quite good enough.

The funny thing about it is that all these kids had those fears and many had a ton of baggage they were trying to carry all by themselves, because they didn't believe anyone else would understand or care. Now they all know differently and will probably never look at life the same. We have kept in touch on Facebook via our team group pages as well as the camp page and, from what I can see, everyone is doing great.

Three of the teens—who indicated they had also been victims of sexual abuse when they were small—had approached me for information on the Victor Walk and Little Warriors. They said that although they had been receiving therapy, they felt that helping others find their voices and feel less alone would be a great addition to what they were already doing. Nothing heals hurt more than helping others through by lending a hand.

A few weeks after I returned home, I was contacted by one of the other camp leaders. His nineteen-year-old brother had just told his family about being abused at the hands of his father when he was young. The problem was they felt helpless; they didn't know where to turn, and not just to help him, but to get through their feelings of helplessness and their guilt of not having been aware of the problem.

So many people are affected by this crime, not just the victims. Sexual abuse shatters our vision of the world as we know it into little tiny pieces and often we will need help to put those pieces back together again. I like to think there is a reason for everything happening, a reason that I attended that camp and a reason that each of the students attended. My hope is that because of that camp and hearing my story, perhaps one person will be inspired to make a career out of helping others or changing the laws to ensure harsher penalties. Who knows what is possible? I do know that these kids are our future and if real change is going to happen, it will happen at their hands.

THE TAKEAWAY LESSON

Never underestimate the impact that your actions and words can have on other people. Deep down, we all crave acceptance and belonging.

Be Brave Ranch

Once I returned from the RYPEN camp, life pretty much went back to normal. I was fairly busy at work and managed to keep myself occupied and out of trouble. The end of October rolled around and as usual, Mom and Dad were heading out to spend the winter in Arizona. Other than that, nothing too exciting was happening.

I began to wonder when we would be seeing Glori again and had really been hoping that an announcement that the Alberta Government would help fund the ranch was coming soon. Glori was fairly tight-lipped and would only say to stay tuned; she would let us know as soon as she knew anything.

Heather, Alison, and I got in touch with Torre—the lady who had coordinated the Lethbridge Victor Walk—and asked her if she would like to join us every other week for informal meetings at my house to discuss upcoming initiatives, plan the next Victor Walk, and also provide support to each other when needed.

The thought for this had come about during one of the downtimes when there really wasn't anything by way of an announcement or an event going on. It was during one of those downtimes that I began to realize that the effects of my abuse, whether I chose to acknowledge them or not, were very real and needed to be addressed. It was almost like I was finally safe to let my guard down. I had no more secrets to hide, no fear of what would happen if anyone knew. The aftermath that I had hidden for so many years had slowly started to show itself to me.

I have spent many hours in silent reflection over the events of my life and how I feel about them and also how I handled them. Now, for the first time that I could remember, I was feeling really angry. I just wanted to scream, swear, yell, cry; to do something to pay tribute to the emotions that I had stuffed so far down in my years of hiding. I was quite surprised about the appearance of all these emotions, taken aback really. What the hell was I supposed to do with all that now? What I wanted more than anything was to talk to others who had also experienced the same things; I wanted support.

Many people go through therapy for these types of things in an effort to reconcile past events with their lives today. I did not want therapy; I wasn't ready for that yet. I had only just acknowledged that this had affected me at all. In my mind, therapy would send a message to myself that I had lost the battle and my abuser had won. I realize that nothing could be further from the truth, but that was how my subconscious was processing it all.

What I did have—and was feeling comfortable with acknowledging—was a deep desire to talk, to release, and to feel connected with others. Normally, I would have chosen to talk to my mom or Lou about whatever it was that was eating me. But this time I felt like what I needed was just someone to listen as I worked through these emotions and the reasons for having them. I did not want someone to make it all better, or to make my problems disappear, or to tell me to do this or that in an effort to help me to stop experiencing what I did.

I embraced my past and along with it finally came the emotions that were attached to it and that was all right: they needed to be felt, and they had earned their freedom. It had taken me so many years to find the courage to lay my cards on the table for the whole world to see. I had found that, since doing so, I immersed myself in helping the cause, raising awareness, getting to know the folks at Little Warriors, and following all the latest news of people like Theo Fleury.

Was I distracting myself? Probably. These were good places for me to focus my energy for sure, but was I avoiding myself in the process? I had attended the Little Warriors prevention and awareness workshop in Coaldale (www.register.littlewarriors.ca/

prevention_program/schedule.html) as well that summer, so all in all, I had distracted myself very much. Now that there was a lull, the only thing that I had to focus on was myself, and I don't think I was quite ready for that yet. Regardless, the emotions came and went at will. The only thing that I could do was to allow them to come and to explore each of them as they did.

Torre, Heather, Alison, and I started meeting as a group every other Tuesday for a few evening hours. Those meetings provided another distraction for me and, since none of us had gone through a support system, we had nothing to model our evenings around; no structure, just random discussion. Anyway, discussion was a good place to start so that's what we did. It allowed me to get to know Torre better and to see that she felt much like I had at the start of this year: on the outside looking in, and wanting to be a part of the whole movement that promised to change the face of how we as a society look at child sexual abuse and the options available to help us in our journeys to heal.

We finally got the date for the next Little Warriors announcement: to be held at the site for the Be Brave Ranch on November 28, 2013. I invited Torre to come with me this time since Heather would not be able to get the time off work. We assumed that this announcement was being made because the approval for funding had finally come. Everyone looked forward to attending and being witness to such a pivotal moment in Little Warriors' history.

Right around the same time, Theo's assistant Dawn contacted Heather and Alison to set the date for Theo to come and help Alison light her tree. Everyone was totally blown away that Theo would be keeping his promise and, even though he had said he would, we'd all thought that it probably wouldn't happen. Well, that's not entirely true. Alison was pretty sure that Theo would come and support her; she has a funny way of getting the impossible to happen.

Prior to the phone call from Dawn, Alison had been thinking that she might want to put off her tree event until late December or possibly January since she had been so busy with school and life lately. And also because she was worried that her event would get lost in the shuffle of Christmas and so many other charity events.

As it turned out, the best date for Theo to come was December 5, so if this was going to happen, we had to pull it together in a hurry. How would we do this? What did we need? Where could we go that could serve as a place to have Theo talk? Nobody really knew what Theo had planned. Was he staying the night? Did he expect to talk to a group of people? We all had very little experience in putting something like this together and to add to that we also had very little time to do it in. We wanted to be able to put something together so that Theo could speak and yet we didn't want to take away any of the donations that were raised in order to pay for a fancy venue and catering.

We had to keep reminding ourselves of the goal of the event: to raise awareness and money for the Be Brave Ranch. Theo wasn't doing this for publicity or to serve as a speaking engagement for himself; he was doing it to support Alison and that was absolutely incredible.

We needed to start planning right away and in the middle of it all was a trip to Edmonton for the Little Warriors announcement.

On the morning of November 27, Torre, Alison, and I started out on yet another road trip; again, Heather had to stay at home to work; she was not at all happy about missing it; and my mom had already left for Arizona for the winter. So it was just the three of us. Road trips without my mom are just not the same: no cookies or Welsh cakes or little sandwiches; just Tim Hortons coffee and the road and only Alison to banter with.

We had a tote full of blankets that my mom had made for the kids who would be visiting the ranch as part of the "Wrap Them In Love" initiative, and a blanket that Alison had made for Glori. Each child who goes to the ranch gets to pick out a blanket that will be theirs to keep and hopefully provide them with comfort in the future when they need it. The blankets and quilts will all be made by someone who wants the children to know that they are special and that someone out there cares very much about them.

We were all pretty excited for the announcement and although we had a pretty good idea of what was going on, Glori had managed to remain pretty tight-lipped about the whole thing. Alison was particularly excited since she would be spending the next summer there as an employee. She would also be having one of the rooms dedicated to her and was allowed to help decorate it. She had been piecing together memorabilia that she planned to hang in the room such as her poster that Theo had autographed at the Victor Walk.

The roads were pretty clear, but it was quite cold outside especially once the sun went down. We hit Red Deer and it was then that Torre finally asked me if I could somehow stop the cold air from blowing on her in the passenger seat. What? Cold Air? There were dual heat controls in my vehicle and her side was set really hot, like 30.5° Celsius; there was no way that she should be cold.

I reached over and felt the air coming out of the vents on her side and, sure enough, not only was it not as hot as it should have been, it was freaking ice cold. Torre was completely frozen. She could no longer feel her feet and they were painfully cold. The tough little bird had not complained once up until that point, and I'm sure she had been in agony!

I turned off the heat on the passenger side hoping that the air would stop blowing. It did not. I tried to direct my vents to blow warm air on her and that helped somewhat but the cold air that blew on her feet just wouldn't stop.

By the time we reached the hotel in Sherwood Park, I imagined that Torre would step out and blocks of ice would be covering her feet. She was actually in pain and I felt so badly for her but there was little I could do except get us checked in as fast as I could so that she could run her feet under warm water in the tub.

Feeling worn out from the drive and the excitement of nearly freezing my new friend to death, plus the pending announcement about the ranch, we decided to call it an early night and actually went to sleep—no giggling, steam rollers, snorting, or hysterical laughter—just sleep. Now I won't point any fingers or anything, but it appears that bedtime shenanigans only occur when Mom is around. Coincidence? I think not!

We woke early the next morning and grabbed coffee and a bite to eat at the Tim Hortons near the hotel, then made our way out to find the ranch with the directions that we'd been given. The actual location of the ranch was fairly secret, so that children who attend it can heal in a safe place; no perpetrators allowed. Torre's feet were still a little tender from the freezing that they'd endured the night before, but now that we were aware of the problem we directed all of the front heat in her direction and covered her feet with a jacket to protect them from the cold air that was still blowing directly on them.

The drive to the ranch site was so pretty. There had been a thick frost the night before and the trees were still covered in it. Sunlight shining on them gave the appearance of a heavenly outdoor wonderland. We arrived at the ranch and immediately the whole dream was real: the ranch would be a reality come hell or high water.

"Wow" does not even begin to describe what we were feeling when we pulled up; there are no words for that; none at all. Here we were in front of the soon-to-be Be Brave Ranch; this was really happening!

We ventured inside and were greeted by Glori and Randi, who is her personal assistant, and the rest of the die-hard ranch supporters. Glori greeted us all with welcoming hugs and took us on an impromptu tour of the main building. Every single room was filled to the brim with beds and chairs and mattresses and a variety of other furniture, which, she told us, had been donated to the ranch by a local company. Glori had not been able to tell anyone about it just yet; she had many wonderful secrets to tell that were all just bubbling up inside.

We unloaded our blankets and set them up on a table so that photos could be taken and then posted to encourage others to make some more. The big room, where the media release would take place, had an outside wall pretty much full of windows, so you could see the trees outside all covered in thick, beautiful frost; the scene was magnificent.

My mind was busy racing about how many children this facility could help. Children who would no longer need to turn to drugs, alcohol, self-harming, and suicide as a means of desperately trying to cope with the crimes committed against them. Instead, they will receive the support they need in order to live their lives to the fullest. The help that is given at this ranch may be exactly what is needed in order for these children to start off on the right foot and make healthy decisions that are no longer based on fear, pain, and anger.

I truly believe that children are not bad. They are sad and hurt and frustrated and misunderstood and, yes, sometimes they are angry; but they are not bad, not unless all else fails and they are left with no choice other than to survive however they can, turning their backs on the world that has forsaken them.

Glori gathered all the supporters who were in attendance and invited them to join her downstairs in the old gymnasium for a smudging. I had never taken part in an Aboriginal ceremony before, so I had no idea what to expect. We formed a large circle and Glori started out by welcoming us all to the ranch. Then she explained that the smudging would help to cleanse the site and release any bad spirits or negative energies that remained there.

The spiritual leader lit sage grass and then blew on it so that it smouldered and gave off a steady stream of smoke. From inside the circle, she went to each person and offered them cleansing. If that person desired, she would wave the smoke toward the person using an eagle feather and the person would then move the smoke over themselves by directing it with their hands over their heads, torsos, and arms.

I was standing beside Halie, the little girl who had sold lemonade to raise money for the ranch. When the elder finished with Halie, Halie made a small nod with her head and said, "Hai, hai." When I asked her later what that meant, she thought it was similar to saying thank you.

Throughout all this ceremony my soul spot just below my breastbone was aching; it felt like a magnet was pulling it gently outward. I have come to know that feeling very well: it means that I am on the right track and to keep on going. That is the same feeling I felt when I knew that I had to go to Ottawa for the Victor Walk. You don't mess with the soul spot, not ever. The ranch ceremony touched me so deeply that I felt as though each of us in that room would forever be connected by that sacred moment and that good things could only come in the future when they started out like that.

We made our way back upstairs and all converged in the big room where cameras were set up ready to capture Glori's big announcement. "This will be the home of the Little Warriors' Be Brave Ranch. It is nestled on 120 beautiful acres and it is 64,000 square feet of space that will need to be renovated with love."

For five months, the Alberta Government had refused to give the funding and because the government wasn't involved, people wouldn't give anymore. Glori told us that when the funding had been refused she literally bawled hysterically. Glori and her board at Little Warriors vowed then that they would build it, no matter what, with or without the government's support.

Glori began speaking again to the crowd, "Today that dream became a reality, because the site with all its buildings has been purchased outright using donations made by Everyday Albertans. It was made a reality by the generosity of kids like the young girl who raised $500 selling lemonade and Alison who raised $10,000 by selling sponsorships to light bulbs, and other Albertans who donated. The facility has been built for love of our children, government money or no government money. There is nothing more amazing than Albertans getting together to say, 'This is the right thing to do and we're going to do it, no matter what.' The dream that was set in motion five-and-a-half years ago is coming true today."

The week that Glori was told that the government would not help fund the beds, she also got a phone call from a woman called Eileen LaBonte who had heard about the situation, was concerned that what had happened was not right, and was going to help make it right. She would donate $1 million in the name of her husband, Ray LaBonte, to the "Be Brave Ranch." A month later, two anonymous angels who had been touched personally as a couple by the cause donated another one million dollars.

The biggest secret Glori had kept was that five months earlier they had raised all the money needed to purchase the facility. "Under the leadership of Dr. Peter Silverstone, a psychiatrist and professor with the University of Alberta, along with about seven experts also from the University of Alberta, a one-year, world-renowned program has been developed, and this facility will be the first long-term treatment centre in the world for kids who have been sexually abused. It will be called the 'Be Brave Ranch' by Ray LaBonte and Family, and it will be *built right here!*' Glori excitedly proclaimed as she pointed to the very space that we were standing in.

Dr. Silverstone spoke about the different facets of the program and how they planned to use many different methods of therapy in order to reach all the children in ways that would speak to them as individuals with individual needs. This program will change the trajectory of children who often end up suffering from depression and anxiety in the short term, but also, sadly, are likely to be affected in the long term by issues such as drug addiction and suicide. There is no doubt as to the positive outcomes that will be seen because of this facility, and our children will finally be given a place to heal. The first two years of programming will be a trial to provide a benchmark to measure the effectiveness of the program to justify applying for future government funding.

After Dr. Silverstone spoke, Glori asked Brandi, who is a very dear friend of Glori's as well as the mother of Halie, the young girl who had the lemonade stand, to speak.

"I have a very unique perspective in this battle. I am a survivor of child sexual abuse. I am also the parent of a child affected by child sexual abuse. I know all too well the true cost of what happens when children have their innocence taken from them far too early by people we thought we knew. Innocence, self-esteem, pride, and value ripped unexpectedly in the most vile ways by people we thought we knew. After my abuse, I spent the next thirty years of my life healing, finding reprieve in claiming back the parts of myself that I thought had been stolen.

"Then, almost three years ago, I had the privilege of choosing an amazing six-year-old daughter through adoption. I was well aware that sexual abuse was a very definite possibility, but it was not confirmed. I chose her anyway despite her trauma. My daughter truly is my hero. She has bravely faced investigations and depositions, counselling and testing; she has endured nightmares and flashbacks, setbacks and breakthroughs. She has gone through suicidal moments and times of trying to hurt herself or others. She struggles daily with trust and safety, but has never ever struggled for a second to love, to accept, to smile.

"Many of you have become very familiar with that smile as you see her commercial on TV or her face on the side of city buses in Edmonton. She chose to do this to help. I have never pushed her ever. She wants to do it to show other kids that it is okay to talk, to be brave, to be a Victor, to stop being a victim, and to end the secrets. Regardless of her issues and pain, she chooses to help anyway.

"Glori has asked me to speak about what this ranch means to kids, kids like my daughter, and kids like me once and why this ranch is so important. I could literally be here all day going on about all the ways that this ranch will help. It may literally mean the difference between life and death. It will invariably save the life of at least one person who would have ended their life of pain in suicide. Now with the hope that this ranch will bring, it will mean a long life of healing themselves and, in various other ways, it will heal others as well. It will mean a chance for addictions to be reduced dramatically. Kids will find their self-esteem in the ashes of their past, standing tall and smiling all over again.

"The Be Brave Ranch will give these broken children the tools that they need to deal with the trauma. It will be a place where kids ostracized by peers over behaviours or rumours find acceptance; where no one judges or blames them; where all the broken pieces can be put back together again by all the beautiful therapists. It will mean healing in their childhood instead of waiting for adulthood, like I did and Glori did. The ranch will bring light where there was once only shadow. It will mean better relationships with parents, family, and friends, and down the road in marriages, relationships, and with themselves. The ranch will bring hope, healing, and empowerment to countless children who would have otherwise been lost one way or another. It will centralize all the therapies and treatments to one location, speeding up the healing and decreasing the stress on both the children and their parents, and, trust me, that's a huge stress. The Be Brave Ranch will be a place for parents and caregivers to come and look up for the very first time since the disclosures started.

"We as parents put our heads down, nose to the grindstone, shutting out the world in an attempt to cope and deal, and we often forget that others can understand and offer support, other parents who walk this same nightmarish road. It will mean that kids will have the chance to be kids again, and that parents will have the chance to see their kids smile again, really truly smile. You never know what kind of a gift that is until it is taken from your child. Parents and kids will be given the gift of knowing how to deal with life when memories come, instead of shutting down or acting out. The Be Brave Ranch will mean that kids who feel like throwaways will feel like they matter, and just like Halie, they will know that somebody chose to help anyway.

"Even though this is such an amazing accomplishment, this ranch, this day and all that it means, it's not enough. I made a promise to myself, to my kids, and to the world, six months ago on the steps of our legislature. I spoke and I vowed to stand for these kids and this ranch until it was a reality. Here I am, standing on this day that it becomes a reality, and I for one don't plan on sitting down anytime soon. I will continue to stand, to fight and to speak up until all these beds are funded, kids are being healed, and lives are being changed.

"We have accomplished so much. We still need to do more. Please continue to stand with us and stand by these amazing kids. It is said that if you teach a man to fish, he will eat for a lifetime. So just close your eyes and visualize for one moment what would happen if you could heal a child affected by child sexual abuse. That will be the real miracle that will happen right here on this ground that we stand on today.

"Thank you from the bottom of my heart, as a survivor, as an advocate, and mostly as a mom."

Once Brandi had finished her speech, Glori took over the microphone once more to fill everyone in on some of the other secrets she had been keeping. She let us know that they had been selling naming rights for a facility that they didn't even have yet, people were just acting on faith. There are a total of six houses at the ranch and Glori's closest friends and supporters had already sponsored four of them. Enbridge had sponsored the library; Executrade had sponsored a room; the garden would be called "Karen's Garden" after a woman whose life ended too short due to sexual abuse; and DynaLIFE sponsored the zipline and obstacle course. There are sixty rooms available to sponsor and the facility will be putting through approximately one hundred kids per year for the first two years. As this is an outcome-based facility, they will need to raise money to put the kids through the next two years of the research phase; there is still a need to raise a lot of money.

So far that morning, a couple had donated $120,000 that will be used to put the first few kids through. They plan to have a lovers' lane so that when the kids go through on horseback they will see signs with, "You Are Loved By Global," "You Are Loved by Randi," etcetera on them. Also there will be a sponsor wall that will say, "You Are Loved By" listing all the sponsors' names underneath. There will be a wishing well on site and the kids will each get two coins when they arrive; one will be to make a wish for themselves and the other will be their wish for the next kids who come. Glori had also told Theo the night before that there was a skating rink and once it is renovated, it will be dedicated to him and called "Theo Fleury's Rink of Courage."

Once the results from the first two years of programming are available, they will go back to the government and say, "Now you have to fund us; we have outcomes."

Glori told the group that none of her blood family, aside from her husband and kids, were in the room because her family had been torn apart by her abuse. She considered her family to be all of her GSquared people and Little Warriors family and the LaBontes and Brandi and all her supporters.

She then continued to talk about the overwhelming generosity and support that had been shown by the donations from a large North American construction company Kiewit, which encompassed $300,000 in furniture items including fifty beds, fifty TVs, fifty garbage cans, dining suites, plus many more items that completely filled the main floor of the big building. In addition, a modern furniture store in Edmonton, Scandia Furniture, had donated $40,000 for furniture.

Glori instructed everyone to check out the Little Warriors website (www.littlewarriors.ca) for a complete list of what is still needed; the names of people and companies who have already taken care of certain items is also posted there.

Glori finished her talk and then guided everyone around the main facility and outside and over to one of the houses on the property. We came back inside the main building after the tour and visited with some of the supporters for a while.

I took a minute to call my mom and tell her where I was and what had been announced. She was overcome with happiness not only for Little Warriors, but for all the children who would be able to receive the help that had not been available to me or my family when I was a child. We both stood and cried tears of happiness and relief over the realization that this ranch is a reality

I hung up the phone and then went outside to meet up with Torre. I could see she was very emotional as well. We hugged and she told me that she was so thankful to have been included in this announcement and thankful that finally there would be a place where kids could heal without having to endure what she had as a child. Back inside, sharing in the happiness and crying right beside all of us were Kerry Towle and Danielle Smith from the Wildrose Party, a conservative provincial political party in Alberta. They were there not for the cameras, but because they have been big supporters and have really big hearts. In fact, they support this cause so much that the Wildrose Party opted to donate the 8 percent pay raise that the Wildrose Party Caucus was set to receive to the Wild Rose Caucus charity fund. Their first donation would be to Little Warriors to help with starting up the Be Brave Ranch and that donation amounted to $25,000.

Talk about our leaders investing back into their people!

Danielle Smith wanted Alison and Brandi and Halie to go to the legislature for a question and answer session. She hoped to be able to introduce us and read the speech that Brandi had read at the ranch. Alison, Torre, Brandi, Halie, and I drove from the ranch to the legislature building, excitedly anticipating what Danielle Smith would have to say about her experience at the ranch that morning.

This was my first time visiting the legislature building in Edmonton and I had no idea what to expect. My first impression upon entering the large building was awe at the level of opulence that surrounded us. Quickly following that awe, however, was an unexpected level of anger at the amount of upkeep and resources that would be required to keep all the ornate fixtures and marble gleaming as they did. I felt incredible resentment toward our government, both past and present, for the sheer waste of taxpayers' hard-earned money.

I was angry that while our children are in such desperate need of a place to heal, funding was not being given for that. And yet everywhere I looked, I could see precious tax dollars being flushed down the toilet, all in the name of pageantry and show. Prior to entering the chambers, our purses and phones had to be checked in at a desk that was set just outside the entrance to the upper balcony observation area where we would be viewing the proceedings. Although the attendants of that desk were fairly polite, I couldn't help but notice that there were three attendants working that small station, two too many from where I stood.

We entered the observation area and from where we sat we had a direct view of the official opposition side of the floor. We were almost directly across from where Danielle Smith was seated and she gave us all a small welcoming wave.

We sat quietly waiting for the question and answer session to begin. Although we sat quietly, inside I continued to stew in my outrage over the extravagance of it all. I watched as the young pages walked to and fro holding their tiny trays, which delivered notes across the floor to members on the other side, or the occasional bottle of water. Alison remarked that she wished she lived in Edmonton so she would be eligible for a job as a page, since it was a relatively high paying job at thirteen dollars an hour, in comparison to the minimum wage of retail or fast food positions; she could then also observe the proceedings on a regular basis.

The schedule was thrown off due to a premier visiting from another province, and the start of the question and answer session was delayed. Although we were able to watch for quite some time, we were unable to stay long enough to see if Danielle was able to read out Brandi's speech that she'd delivered earlier at the ranch.

What we did see was Danielle Smith call on Alberta's Premier Redford to fund our beds at the ranch out of the victims-of-crime fund, which reportedly currently held a surplus of over $50 million. We watched as she announced defiantly to the Progressive Conservatives that they needn't worry about funding, because Albertans were stepping up and contributing out of their own pockets and that Little Warriors will fund it anyway. She announced that she had just come from the ranch where the opening had been announced. I was very surprised to see the level of support that her comments received from the rest of the assembly as they banged away on their tables and cheered. A great end to a great day for sure!

THE TAKEAWAY LESSON

When you dream, dream big; and when you want that dream to become a reality, take action toward it. Nothing ventured, nothing gained!

Let There Be Light!

With only days remaining before Theo would be coming to help Alison light her tree for her "Shed Some Light" on child sexual abuse campaign, there was much to do. We were feeling overwhelmed and worried that we might not be able to attract the same level of financial support that the previous year's campaign had attracted. Alison had started working part-time at a local fast food outlet and her spare time was very limited. Heather, Torre, and I worked hard at getting Alison's posters ready, as well as preparing flyers that would be dropped into grocery bags at a grocery store in Coaldale. The town had also promised to put a notice in with the utility bills for the month as well. Heather booked the Coaldale Community Centre for the evening of the tree lighting, so we would have a place for everyone to congregate afterward.

The previous year's tree lighting was very low key, attended only by Alison's parents, her bother, and five of her close friends, which was in my opinion, a very small show of support relative to the fact that she had raised $10,000. In addition to that, the lighting of the tree was held on the same night that a Christmas parade of lights was held. That parade had brought roughly 10,000 people to the town, but sadly most of those people just bypassed her event. This year we would try our best to beat that goal of $10,000 from the year before and hopefully get some additional community support and publicity for the event; ultimately the goal is to raise awareness and get people talking about child sexual abuse.

When Torre, Alison, and I were in Edmonton for the announcement at the ranch, Heather had picked up a couple of Calgary Flames hockey jerseys, one for auctioning and one for

Alison for Christmas. When I dropped Alison off at her house after our Edmonton trip, Heather was so excited about the jerseys that she came out to show them to us. I hoped that Heather was right and that we could raise some money through auctioning off a Calgary Flames hockey jersey, but I have to admit that in the back of my head I was worried that it might not go over as well as we had hoped.

With so little time to pull everything together, we knew it would not be the gala event that Alison had envisioned. We were constantly reminding ourselves that, even though Theo was attending, he was there to support the cause and raise awareness for child sexual abuse; he was not expecting a big, fancy event. To tell you the truth, I was beginning to feel awfully discouraged at the lack of support we were getting. Here we had a great cause; everyone in the town of Coaldale had been given notices with their utility bill statements; and yet we were struggling to get people to attend. We even had the local radio stations announcing it and Alison had done interviews for the local paper as well. There was a hockey tournament being held at the same time as our event in an adjacent building; however, that did nothing to add to our attendance. This really pointed out just how uncomfortable people are about discussing child sexual abuse. We had an ex-NHL player and celebrity right next door to a big hockey tournament, and yet, we saw nobody from that tournament attend.

I had sent out an email asking for support from a couple of lawyers in Lethbridge whom I often worked with in real estate transactions. One of them not only offered to sponsor bulbs, he also sent the message out to all his colleagues who were part of the Lethbridge Bar and asked them to consider supporting as well. I heard back from two lawyer's offices out of the many that were petitioned for support, but that was all. Because Theo was going to be there, we originally expected to be able to get a large number of people out to the hall that night. We had to have a ticket system to attend the meet and greet with Theo, to keep track of numbers in case we had too many people for the fire code at the hall, but we kept the fee low at $10 to attract more people. We thought that the cost was more than fair, since people would pay up to $300 for a seat at other fundraisers that Theo attended. It was like pulling teeth to get people to come out.

There came a point when we needed to make a decision based on the low support for the meet and greet. We had to keep it simple, low key—dessert squares, hot chocolate, coffee, and water. Heather was able to get a local flower shop, The Blooming Willow, to donate all the centrepieces for the tables. We purchased plastic tablecloths for the tables and sprinkled some tree-shaped confetti on each of them. Alison and Heather decorated the hall, while Heather and I, along with two others, set up the tables and made coffee and hot chocolate. A few members of the girls' hockey team came out to help pass out desserts, and one of Alison's close friends manned a table for donations at the door. It wasn't much, but it was the best we could do given the circumstances.

As luck would have it, the night of the tree lighting was one of the coldest nights we had all winter. I mean it was bitter, freaking cold, like minus 30° plus wind chill. The Town of Coaldale donated a tree beside the town office and volunteers hung the white lights on it. The tree was huge, probably one of the biggest ones on that street for sure. We finished up at the community centre and made our way over to the town office for the lighting of the tree. Everyone huddled inside their vehicles while we waited for Theo to arrive, hoping that we would have more people show up as the time to light the tree drew closer. Theo played it smart and met the press inside the town hall for his and Alison's interviews. As soon as we saw them come out of the town office, everyone hopped out of their vehicles and converged in front of the tree.

One really cool moment for me was when Theo first walked down the sidewalk toward the tree—he immediately recognized me and came over and gave me a big hello hug. It felt just like the kind of hug you get from a brother you haven't seen in years, genuine and glad to see each other. Not only was that really cool to experience, but it also nailed down that feeling of us all being in this together, one big Victor family if you will.

The lights on the tree had not been tested that day, so there was a small moment of worry that they would not light and we had our fingers crossed inside our jacket pockets. A switch inside the town office building controlled the lights on the tree and we had Alison's little brother Jonah waiting beside that switch for Theo to give the command. As we watched the tree with Alison and Theo standing beside it, Theo yelled back to Jonah, "Let there be light!" Jonah flipped the switch and voila! The tree lit up with one thousand light bulbs, each representing a victim of child sexual abuse. It was a very much-anticipated moment and in that second, everything that had hiccupped in the planning and every negative emotion we had experienced dissolved away in the light of that beautiful tree.

There are moments in everyone's life where things just seem to come together, to make sense. For me, this was one of them. I felt so full of happiness to have been able to be a small part of that event and I am looking forward to whatever comes in 2014. We all headed over to the community centre for dessert and the meet and greet with Theo. It would be wonderful to get out of the cold and warm up a bit.

We allowed a few minutes for everyone to arrive and then started the evening with a donation to Little Warriors from the Kinsmen Club of Coaldale who presented a cheque and took some photos. Next, Alison's little sister Abigail gave a beautiful tribute to Alison; it was written very well and showed just how much she looked up to her big sister and was very proud of her. I could hear Theo whisper "Wow" sitting beside me. It's so nice to witness when siblings show support for each other.

As emcee, Heather introduced everyone, which was great,

because I didn't have a clue what we were doing or who was speaking when. Next I said a few words about what it had meant to me personally to meet Alison. I was glad to be able to thank her for that and for introducing me to such a great bunch of people who all support the same goal of ending the shame. Alison always has her eyes set on the goal of building the Be Brave Ranch and I don't think she realized that being a part of the past year's events had also provided me with a sense of belonging, of no longer being alone. She has inspired me to do what I can to raise awareness as well.

I introduced Alison to the people in attendance and she spoke about how much this dream meant to her, as well as to so many other children who are in need of healing. She spoke of how the Be Brave Ranch will be able to provide the immediate healing and extensive therapy that these young victims need in order to move past their pain and begin to enjoy just being kids again. She thanked everyone for coming out and then introduced Theo.

In true Theo style, he captivated the audience with many of the same stories that I had heard him talk about twice before—at the Victor Walk and also at the ad campaign for the Be Brave Ranch. It didn't matter how many times I heard the stories that he told: they still caught my full attention. One of the best parts of his talk was when he challenged the Mayor of Coaldale to get his town involved, telling them that if they were really interested in putting Coaldale on the map, they would wrap the whole damn town in lights the next year in support of Alison and her tree to raise awareness of child sexual abuse.

Theo told the crowd how those of us who have been sexually abused as children refer to ourselves as Victors. He told how everything he has done in the past was, in his eyes, a platform for him to be able to be the voice of so many for people to listen to what he has to say.

Somehow, the public is open and supportive when they hear about the hardships of a celebrity. Such an awareness provides people with the hope that great things are possible even in the aftermath of adversity. Theo talked about the importance of raising awareness to this topic and removing the shame surrounding it.

Something that really caught my attention during his talk was a topic that I hadn't heard him talk about before. He shared how he had struggled to get the help that he needed through therapy and he encouraged everyone, especially males, to talk about the feelings they were left with as a result of their abuse. For him, it took a long time to be able to cry, to just really open up and let it all out.

Males in our society are taught that crying is a sign of weakness, whereas actually the opposite is true. It takes incredible strength to trust someone enough to open yourself up and acknowledge the emotions you feel. If we hold our grief in and do not allow ourselves to release it, it often will surface as anger and self-destruction. He talked about how that was the case with him. He started drinking and doing drugs in order to help himself keep numb to all he had gone through. His relationships with his wives and kids suffered and his career suffered. Once he was able to face his past, then he was able to let go and begin to heal.

He pointed out to the crowd that happiness is possible and used Alison, Heather, and me as examples, telling the crowd to look at us: we were up there smiling and enjoying life and doing what we could to help others do the same.

After Theo had finished speaking, Alison presented him with a fruit bouquet, which she thought was appropriate because he was "on a health kick." She had also something special to give Theo, something that meant very much to all of us Victors. We knew Theo hates to receive gifts, I mean really; but Alison just couldn't let him come all that way to support her and the cause, the way that he did, and send him on his way without showing how extremely grateful we all were, especially Alison. The year 2013 had been an incredible year for all of us, and that was a direct result of finding our voices as Victors and belonging to that greater community.

Heather and Alison had a friend, Tanya Wurzer, who with the help of her husband and son was able to create a Christmas ornament with their commercial scroll machine. The ornament was oval-shaped and it had the Victor frog etched on it along with "2013." The idea was to give Theo something that would commemorate the year for the inaugural Victor Walk and the start of the Victor Movement. We knew he would enjoy it, but none of us expected him to be as blown away as he was. He held the ornament up for the crowd and exclaimed, "Wow! This is awesome! Really cool!"

He went on to tell the crowd how he absolutely hated getting gifts—always had and always would—but this gift would be something that he would treasure. It would be something that he could hang on his tree every year and be reminded of where it all began. He looked over at us and asked if we thought he should explain its meaning and, when we all agreed that he should, he went on to explain to everyone the significance of the ornament and why we called ourselves Victors and why the mascot is a frog. He told the story about how often the frog popped up and what it symbolizes in the Aboriginal culture. Alison was thrilled that he responded so well to the gift. It really was a perfect way to show her thanks to Theo, one of her biggest heroes.

Once Theo finished talking, Alison began to auction off the Calgary Flames jersey that Heather had picked and he had worn during the evening, along with a copy of Theo's book, *Playing With Fire*. The bidding started out pretty slowly. Alison didn't want to appear greedy and so she started out just trying to make a wee bit more money than the jersey was purchased for. Then two bidders began to jockey for the highest bid. It was going well, the interest was there, but Alison hesitated to raise the bid price each time. Theo jumped in to give her a hand and within minutes the jersey and autographed book had sold for $2,000!

Now that was incredible, but what happened next was even more heartwarming. The winning bidder donated the jersey and book back so that the process could begin again and we could raise more money for the Be Brave Ranch. Theo graciously offered to provide each of the top bidders with a jersey and so now instead of $2,000, we had raised $4,000! I was stunned at the price that was paid, not once, but twice. Just blown away! Even Theo was pumped about the support.

After all the bidding was finished, Theo mingled with the crowd, signed autographs, and took pictures with whoever wanted them. He talked with people about the Be Brave Ranch and what they could do to help and who to contact for more information. I introduced my husband Lou to Theo, and Lou, who was feeling really silly about asking for an autograph, managed to get one of his lacrosse jerseys signed since that was the only thing that he had available. I introduced Theo to my son Tony, who had also come out to support me and the cause that evening. My friend Kristin had come as well and I couldn't have thanked her enough. This is what a true friend does: they support each other in the things that are important, no matter how freaking cold it is, or what else they would rather be doing.

I remember thanking Theo for taking the time to come out and he said again, as I had heard him say before, "Whatever it takes; whatever it takes." Next, I introduced Theo to Torre, the Lethbridge Victor Walk Coordinator, and then I introduced him to a male friend of mine who had recently disclosed his abuse to his family and was having a hard time dealing with the anger he felt, which is really very common.

My friend told Theo that he was trying to get help but that he had learned he would have to go all the way to Calgary or Red Deer to get help specific to child sexual abuse. At first, Theo was shocked and upset, wanting to talk to the politician who was in the building with us. But then he switched gears and suggested that my friend get therapy for *trauma*, since that was what the issue really is. Victims of child sexual abuse are trauma victims and almost every town and city provides services for that. He went on to describe how that was the approach that he and his therapist, Kim Barthel, had been taking lately in dealing with the effects of child sexual abuse and that they were working on replacing those three words with just trauma whenever they could.

My friend thanked Theo and got a picture with him, which he posted on his Facebook page along with a message of thanks to Theo for a night that he would remember forever.

There it was. Such a simple conversation—no big bells and whistles, no fanfare needed. It was just that simple conversation that would allow yet another person to feel a sense of belonging to our ever-growing community of Victors. Above all, I believe, that the sense of belonging is absolutely the most powerful thing to feel. Miracles happen when we release the shame and no longer feel alone, and I had just witnessed a miracle for sure.

While everyone milled around the room, a young lady who had been a great help to us while setting up the room earlier that day called me over to talk. She and her husband wanted to encourage me to continue writing my book and to tell me that they would like a copy of it once it is complete. The reason, she said, was that she was also a victim of child sexual abuse and that I was the first person that she had told other than her husband, and she had only just told him a few days before that.

All I could do was thank her so much for being brave enough to share that with me and hug her tightly. I was so taken aback that she had chosen me to tell her story to and I was having a hard time believing that I was a worthy confidante. I had assumed that she would have wanted to share that with Theo instead. She had chosen me. In a world so full of other people to tell, she had chosen me. I was honoured.

Later when I joined up with Theo, I told him that someone had just shared with me that they had been abused and I was only the second person they had ever told. I don't know why I was so shocked by her telling me, other than that I had never considered myself to be anyone special; just another Victor. Maybe I assumed that people would gravitate toward Theo because he is the celebrity and has the respect of the crowd. At any rate, she chose me and I began to understand that I too have the power to help people release their shame.

When I told Theo about it, without telling him who she was, I remember him looking at me with a kind of look that said, "No shit, silly. What did you expect?" For Theo, it is an everyday occurrence; people send him emails by the thousands and seek him out anytime he is in public. For me, however, this was a new thing; something totally unexpected. I suppose it all goes back to wanting so badly to belong, to share our stories with someone who will understand, someone who has been there, regardless of the reason for it. I prepare myself for that happening more and more often as I continue to be an advocate and share my story with others.

As the crowd started to leave and we began to tidy up the room, Alison put the stereo on so that she could play Theo's "Walk With Thousands" song. We all sang along, happy that the evening was over. It was a very fitting end to a long day. Theo hugged Alison goodbye and then I gave him a hand out to his car with all the items he had to take with him: the centrepiece that we insisted he take back home to his wife Jenn, along with some desserts, his fruit bouquet, and the new ornament.

We talked a little about how I was hoping to write a story about the events of the past year and what they mean to me, and how our small group of Victors had started meeting every other week to offer support to each other. I let him know that I really wanted to help out any way that I could and I hoped that he would one day take me up on that, although I imagine that he has people offering help like that to him all the time.

We loaded his car up and decided to have a smoke together before he went on his way. I told him about how incredible the

Be Brave Ranch is and how I had called my mom from the ranch after the purchase of it was announced and how moved my mom had been at hearing me be a part of it since she was still in Arizona. I suggested that we could really blow her mind if we called her that night and have Theo say hi to her. He agreed, and before you know it my mom was talking on the phone to Theo and I could hear her excitement through the phone. She made sure to tell him to take his time and drive safely home because it was cold and miserable outside. I smiled as Theo promised to take it easy on the way home and told her that he would be fine travelling tonight; he didn't need to stay over and leave in the morning.

Once a mom, always a mom. It doesn't matter who the person is. That role doesn't change. I can remember my mom cheering for Theo during his games with the Calgary Flames. She would call him out by name and talk to him like he could hear her through the television. "Oh, Theo, look out." "There it is, Theo. There it is! Go get it!" and so on. That for me was probably the only way that I had recognized his name prior to the whole Victor Movement. Whether he knew it or not, she had cheered him from the sidelines for years and she was still cheering for him now.

Shane, who is Heather's husband and Alison's dad, came outside with Heather so that they could say their goodbyes as well. Everyone got massive hugs and Shane, who has always silently taken care of things behind the scenes for Heather, for once got to enjoy being a part of this event with a front row seat. It really was about time for Shane and Lou to be at an event and to experience firsthand the joy and the pride that we Victors feel.

Shane supported Alison and Heather by taking care of things at home and by holding down the fort with Alison's two younger siblings all year while they were off at this or that press release etcetera. He often did so without complaining a smidge.

In fact, both Lou and Shane, in my eyes, are the unsung heroes who make everything possible. Lou takes care of our clients and picks up the slack for me in my absence from work. I honestly don't think that Lou fully understood just how much I had needed to be a part of the events in the last several months until that night. When I got home that evening, he was patiently waiting for me with hugs and we started the first of many bigger conversations that would help him understand the role he plays in supporting me and why it is so ultimately important that he does.

I'm happy to report that Alison's Shed Some Light on Child Sexual Abuse Campaign raised $11,500 this year, so that makes it a total of over $20,000 in just two years!

THE TAKEAWAY LESSON

The most satisfying work you can do is to help someone else achieve their dream or reach their goal. Sometimes the biggest heroes are the ones who take the time to show up and encourage others.

Chapter Nine

Excuses

In the weeks following Alison's tree lighting, I couldn't help but notice a recurring theme common among survivors. I could see that many appeared to use their abuse as an excuse for whatever was lacking in their lives. I understand there are reasons we all behave the way we do; I just have a problem when that reason becomes an excuse.

What is the difference between a reason and an excuse? Let's think about that for a minute. Everybody—and I do mean everybody—will face setbacks in life in one form or another. Please don't misunderstand my intentions here; I have to vent on the topic just a little. We are all products of what we have been through in life up to this point. But why is it that some people choose to be the worst possible product instead of the most inspiring one?

Adversity is given in order that we can grow and overcome it, and then to turn the situation around and help others do the same. I have always said that the moment you recognize why you are a certain way is the moment you no longer can use that as an excuse for being that way. From that moment forward, you are given a choice: do you work hard and put your best foot forward always mindful of your shortcomings and how to overcome them? Or do you use that reason as an invisible crutch, an excuse to be lazy and remain as you are?

I know that there are very real behaviours and attitudes as well as mental health issues that are direct results of the adversities that we face. I keep seeing people who hang onto the false belief that the world owes them something for being shortchanged. Guess what? I have news for you. The world owes you nothing! The world owes me nothing!

Are many of us dealing with post-traumatic stress, anxiety issues, anger, and depression? Absolutely! But that doesn't have to be how you define yourself. Life is a long frigging time, and I for one have no intention of reliving my painful past over and over and over, so that it can also determine my future. I will put my foot down right now to beg you to please stop reliving your past. It is actually easier to use our past as an excuse for our lack of happiness today than it is to get off your ass and take a step toward getting yourself healed.

Change doesn't happen overnight for sure, but at the very least, please be willing to take that step forward out of the darkness. Nobody expects you to just go "poof" and feel all better, but please have the courage to work on it. There is no predetermined timeframe involved in healing since each situation is unique, but as long as you hang on tightly to anger, hurt, and betrayal as the crutches that hold you back from living a full and happy life, they will not disappoint.

Don't get me wrong, I understand you may be having a hard time and that's okay, But I for one am sick and tired of sitting around blaming every little thing that is wrong in my life on what I went through as a child. I am done! I see people every day who will walk around with their hand out hoping that someone will feel sorry for them and their situation and take care of them. They are the first people to tell you how hard it is to live through such trauma, but they are doing so well in spite of it all. They take situations that everyone regardless of their background faces every day, and they say, "Oh, poor me!" because they have made poor choices and continue to make them every day!

I have had people look at me and say, "Well, you are lucky. It must be nice to do what you do and have the things that you have." Nothing makes me angrier. I was not born with a silver spoon in my mouth; I also do not expect people to take care of me. I have always worked very hard for everything that I have and have always done so, even when my world was crumbling around me as a young mother. I pushed through then and I push through now and I do so only because I refuse to wait for someone to feel sorry for me and do it all for me.

When I was a single mom, I had a hell of a time making ends meet. I did not receive child support when the kids were small and counted on every penny that I made with my own two hands to feed my children, clothe them, and put a roof over their heads. I am affected by the abuse that I endured as a child; I am affected by the way that I chose to deal with that abuse. I have to live every day with the decisions that I make, not the abuse that I endured. The abuse set into motion some ways of self-protection and some strategies for coping in certain situations. But it is not responsible for my actions today.

Only I can be held accountable for my actions; they are mine, not my abuser's. I own my thoughts and my emotions, and I refuse to let my life be poisoned any further than the actual moments in time that I was actually being abused. I hope that makes sense.

I am constantly learning about myself and I am also constantly surprised by the things that I learn. For example, when I am experiencing higher-than-normal levels of stress, I tend to check out mentally. For me, it means that I can be sitting at a table for hours yet it feels like only minutes have passed. It is not the most productive thing to have to deal with, but it is just what happens when I am feeling overwhelmed.

Until very recently, I had no idea that this, along with many other things that I do, is a symptom of post-traumatic stress disorder, which does actually make a lot of sense. Now that I am aware of why I do what I do, I am also aware that I can work toward changing what I do. The self-preservation techniques that I use are the same ones that I used when I was a child and couldn't protect myself. I am no longer a child and I am more than capable of protecting myself now in most cases; so the need for this response is not immediately necessary. I do not consciously choose to zone out; it's not like I can just say, "Well, that's enough of this shit. I'm going to take a mental moment and check out for a while."

I was not conscious of doing that when I was a child at all. I just remember feeling out of it, and also stupid because I couldn't remember things, and even more stupid because the more that I tried to remember things or learn things, the more stressed out I ended up feeling and therefore the more I would check out and not remember a fricking thing! It was a vicious circle for sure.

In a way, I am relieved to know that I am in fact very intelligent and not just a space cadet! I had such a hard time with math as a kid; I mean a really hard time. The more I tried, the worse I got. Until.... I can remember working in the cash office at a grocery store and working with numbers and not having a problem at all and thinking, "Well, how does that happen? I couldn't put two and two together as a kid, but it doesn't seem that difficult now. That is strange." What I didn't pick up on was that the stress of learning was what I was having a hard time dealing with; it wasn't the numbers at all.

This also conveniently puts an answer to why it was I had such a tough time when writing exams; they seem much easier to write when you are not zoning in and out of reality every couple of minutes. Again though, I stand by my words from earlier: I refuse to let my abuse be the reason for any struggles I go through today. The techniques I subconsciously adopted to get me through trauma as a child have indeed followed me through to my adulthood; but that does not mean I have to accept them as the only way I can handle stress.

My mind reacted as efficiently as it could in order to save the sanity of the child it was trying to preserve. I am an adult now and I have the ability to acknowledge the stress in my life at any given time and to then remove myself from it by choice. I could also retrain myself to use different proven stress-reducing techniques in the place of the old ones that I adopted as a child, if those are hindering my ability to live to the best of my potential.

It is also important to recognize that just because we develop ways to cope as children and carry those coping mechanisms over into adulthood, it doesn't automatically mean that they are inappropriate. Sometimes, those coping techniques serve us very well. What is important is being aware of how we are getting through times of stress or anxiety and determining if that approach is something that works for us anymore.

I was pretty surprised even to figure out that I had been affected at all by the abuse that I had been handed as a child. I had completely fooled myself and I had fooled those around me. I honestly believed I was just fine and had made it through unscathed. Truth be told, I am just fine, and yes, I am still here and in one piece, so I must have made it through for the most part unscathed. I can't help but wonder, though, if that is because I was so determined to be normal and unaffected by any of it. My secrecy depended on my not raising any red flags that might tell the tale of the trauma I was living through.

Now the trauma is over and I am reflecting back on my life, I can see that perhaps there is a place for some therapy, a place where it is safe to investigate what makes me tick the way I do and to learn how I can improve on being a better version of myself in order to help others.

I used to get all worked up over that thought. "Therapy? Ha, not this girl! Didn't need it then; sure don't need it now! Or do I?" How do we know until we try and what is there to lose in trying? What is there to be afraid of? Everyone knows now. There is nothing to hide and only things to gain. It's time to let go of the fear and sail curiously down the river of self-exploration.

Some people experience pretty severe flashbacks and feel extreme anxiety and distress as a result of them. I had never had a real flashback before this year. I had plenty of memories, but when I remembered instances of abuse, I would mentally remove myself from feeling any of the real emotions that had gone along with those memories. The only real exceptions to that are how I feel when I smell some things such as Colgate toothpaste and a certain aftershave.

My memories are intensely related to smells; I can immediately recall the smell of my childhood Dr. Seuss books. Yes, I do mean the smell of the actual paper when I see the pictures or hear part of the book being read. I can feel the comfort I felt as a child having my mom reading us our bedtime story and tucking us in. I also will hear an old song on the radio and be mentally transported back to my childhood, in the back seat of my mom's station wagon where I can smell the way the vinyl headrest of the seat in front of me smelled. I also relate the memory of the emotions from that situation as well; likely because it relates to a positive emotion.

What I had never had until this year was a severe flashback involving a really negative emotion.

Wham!

I was woken up with images and emotions of this flashback in the middle of the night, seemingly out of the blue. I had actually forgotten that any of the items in that flashback had taken place. I had been with Lou for ten years and this was the first he would be hearing about it, not because I didn't want him to know; only because it wasn't anywhere close to being on my radar.

I awoke to myself screaming in my sleep. My heart was pounding and I could not shake the images that filled my mind, the memories I had so successfully forgotten before that night. I got out of bed and went to the window, peering out into the night. I hoped that I could just calm myself enough to get back to sleep. The more I tried to shake the feeling, the worse it got. I went downstairs and continued my meltdown until Lou got up the next morning.

When he came downstairs, I told him all about the flashback and the memory it belonged to. I was so angry at reliving that experience. Lou was visibly shaken and was pressing pretty hard for me to go to a counsellor to talk about what I had been through. I, on the other hand, had no intention of doing that. Lou was not used to seeing me that way, in such a state of raw emotion that bordered on a total and complete breakdown. He finally talked me into reaching out to Theo; he would understand. And I'm sure Lou thought that if Theo said to get my ass into counselling, I might listen.

As it turned out, by the time I sent Theo a message, I was beginning to pull myself together, starting to feel like I was again in control. I had a meeting for work that day and was able to clean up and pull it together enough to attend. I figured by then I was fine and told Theo not to bother.

I look back at that now and wonder why the hell I even agreed to try to connect with Theo. I mean it wasn't that we were buddies or anything. He hardly knew me. I was likely just some groupie fan in his mind. Maybe it was because he approached so much with a level-headed matter-of-factness that I needed at that time. He probably would have said, "Ya, no shit. You need help. Of course you feel like you are having a breakdown. Did you think you could keep it all locked inside and never have it spill out?"

Maybe that is why I just told him I was all right. I already had the answer to this situation in my head and it would have been redundant to ask him for what I already knew; I'm sure he had many other much more productive things to deal with aside from my temporary breakdown. Imagine if everyone dealt with their problems that way, "Oh, hey, I'll just ask Theo. He'll know what to do." What a mess things would be in and poor Theo himself would likely melt down!

Regardless, I had acknowledged the memory and then promptly placed it with the rest of my not-so-happy memories, buried way deep down and out of sight. This time I had allowed myself to cry. It was the first time I had and it felt so good, almost like a soft cleansing rain on a warm spring day. I didn't spend days crying like I had been worried I might end up doing. Instead, I just relinquished some of the emotions I had let build up inside me; that seemed to work for the time being.

In the days and weeks that followed my first real out-of-control flashback, I couldn't help but feel for the other victims who experience those same types of things so often that they are unable to carry on any normal semblance of life. How were they coping? Would therapy even help them? Man, I hope so. There is nothing worse than being crippled by the past so badly that you can no longer live in the moment and have a hard time dreaming of the future.

What I had experienced was very real and no amount of telling me to just get over it would ever have been able to make it go away. The only thing that put that memory back into its hiding spot was my built-in safety mechanism that I had developed so many years ago. Thank God for now that it still worked. The next question is, how long will it work for?

This past year, I have been having to confront many issues that have come up since I let go of my shame. It is almost like a higher power is watching and saying, "All right, now you can handle another bite. When you swallow that bite, I will give you one more."

Having these experiences does not change my feeling that I refuse to be a victim and stay at home and feel badly for myself. What it does do is open my eyes to the fact that, like it or not, I have issues that will need attention sooner rather than later if I want to deal with them from a healthy mindset. In the meantime, I will keep pursuing my passion of helping others through this and will keep writing and speaking about it in the hope that even one other person can relate.

THE TAKEAWAY LESSON

Your past should never be an excuse for your future. Let it inspire you and challenge you. The moment you can understand why it is that you do something a certain way is the very moment that you have the power to move forward differently.

Chapter Ten

What Have I Learned So Far?

So far this year I have experienced some pretty amazing things and I have learned so much about myself in the process. Above all, I have learned that sharing my story with others has given me a newfound sense of empowerment. I have learned that in finding my voice and releasing myself from the lingering feelings of shame around my abuse, I can overcome anything that life throws at me.

Now I'm not saying that in order to heal everyone must speak publicly about his or her abuse, because that would be silly. Some people find it comforting to do that and some people do not.

Victims need to feel like they can talk to someone, anyone who they are comfortable with, and they need to make sure that the people they talk to aren't actually hindering their healing by perpetuating the myth that they should feel guilty about what has happened to them.

Sometimes we are able to talk to close friends and family—which was the case with me—but we still carry the shame that is attached to the abuse and never really let it go. We often continue to feel isolated in our pain and try to hide the true extent of our suffering from those who are close to us.

For as long as I can remember, I have had what I call my "soul spot" guiding me. I describe it as a feeling in my solar plexus that pulls me toward something or pushes me away from something and it feels somewhat like a magnet pulling just under the surface. When I am in tune with that feeling and follow what it is signalling me to do, life works out and the things I need in my life appear.

There have been times I have not listened to my soul spot and things just continually go wrong. I often say that when I am following my soul spot, it is like body surfing naked and I just have to go with wherever it takes me and things work out great. When I ignore those feelings, it feels like I am walking upstream with my nose in the air. Long ago, I learned I should never, ever mess with my soul spot. In fact, I often don't understand why it is I am pulled to do something or be somewhere or call someone until much later when I look back.

For me, every place that I have been to this past year and everything that I have experienced is a direct result of listening to that soul spot. Other than the obvious release of shame and new insights that I have gained into myself and why I do some of the things I do, I have yet to find the big reason for the pull. I do, however, know there is a bigger reason for sure and I am being called to be a part of it.

Maybe it is just about helping others find their voice. Or maybe it is just for the experience and self-growth of it all. Regardless, I will just continue to follow where it leads and see where I end up.

THE TAKEAWAY LESSON

Admitting that we need help and support from others is not a sign of weakness. It means that we are strong and have the courage to do what we need to in order to live full and happy lives.

Chapter Eleven

Coincidence? I Think Not!

For the past several years, I have been writing bits of my story here and there, often finding the process too painful, because I felt I had to dredge up all the emotions and situations that were part of my childhood. I recently thought I could tell the childhood story and finish it off with the story of the last year and how being a part of this bigger picture has made a difference in the way I view myself.

With quite a bit of writing done over the years, I thought it might be time to investigate how to go about publishing, because I could see the end of the book in my sight. I looked at several helpful hints online about how to go about publishing. First, I had investigated the traditional publishing houses, but it looked like getting one of them to pick up the book would be nearly impossible.

For some reason, call it fate, call it my soul spot, I kept searching almost obsessively for answers to how I could get published. I scrolled through the internet for hours, looking for the solution to what I needed in order to get my book out so that other people can read it and be inspired.

I came across a self-publishing company online and filled out my phone number and email, for them to send me information on the packages they had available. After I received the emails they sent me, I spent quite a bit of time pouring through the information. Was this what I was looking for? Was this the answer I needed? I wasn't sure, but what I did know was that if I simply continued to write and do nothing other than register the keystrokes on my computer, there would be no way in the world that what I had written would be able to help anyone.

A few weeks after I had filled in the information requested

on the self-publishing website, I received a call from one of the company's representatives. He wanted to know what my book was about and when I thought I would be finished writing. When I told him about the story and that I thought I would be finished pretty soon, he began to tell me about a special package promotion they had on at the time and how lucky I was that if I signed up with that company right then, I would only have to pay half of what it would normally cost to publish my work.

Now at this point, I had almost resigned myself into accepting that the only way to get published would be to move forward with a self-publishing company, so I have to admit that I was really paying attention to what he was saying. I had a number of questions about the publishing process and what was included in the package, and this guy very patiently tried his best to answer all my questions. After being on the phone with him for close to an hour and a half, I let him know I would need some time to talk with Lou and think things over. He was very accommodating and set up a time for us to talk again the following week.

I sat and thought to myself, "Jeez! What if this is the only way and I put it off too long and miss the sale?" I had no desire to pay double the amount he'd quoted in order to move forward with publishing. The man from that company had also mentioned that I needn't worry about taking my time to finish the book, because I could take as long as I needed and the package would not end up costing me more; they would honour the original contract.

As I mulled my options over in my mind I couldn't help but notice the internal struggle that my soul spot was having. On one hand, the book would be published and that felt right in my soul. So did the fact that I was looking into the publishing process at that time and not waiting until the book was done. In fact, it was almost like I was being pulled to investigate all the avenues right at that time; it consumed me to do so.

On the other hand, even though the fellow on the phone thought that people could be helped by the message in my book, the conversation was focused only on the package, and my soul spot pushed me away from that, leaving a bad feeling in my gut. I knew I needed to get published; I knew I had not found any options that would be any different from the option that was sitting in front of me at that moment. I knew my soul spot had pulled me to do something right away; but why then was I also feeling pulled away from this option? Why then was there that small seed of doubt forming in my mind and nagging at me like a mosquito when you are trying to sleep?

I pondered for the better part of that day what it was that my soul spot was trying to say. There was a message being sent to me for sure, but what was it? I could tell I needed to be searching out a publisher at that time without a doubt, which is why I had felt so compelled to investigate it now, after all the years of writing, and not earlier. I had combed over the internet for hours looking for an answer to my internal pull to get the book published and had come up with that one company. At least I felt good enough about that company to send them my information and spend all that time talking on the phone with their representative. So what was it then that felt off to me?

That evening, as Lou and I made our supper together, I began to talk with him about getting the book published and everything I had learned about the process. I told him how I was absolutely driven toward publishing now and that I felt there was a purpose for my book, even though I did not yet realize what that purpose would be. Lou has been with me long enough to understand that when something pulls at me, there is always a reason and that I never mess with that feeling, not ever!

We talked about the way I had felt pulled to go to Ottawa for the Victor Walk and how that decision had led to all the events and experiences I had had over the past several months. It had also been the same feeling that had led me to sign up for an event that Theo and his therapist Kim Barthel were holding in Calgary in March 2014, which at the time, was called "Conversations in

Healing." When I saw there was an upcoming event, I immediately signed up and booked my hotel; no questions asked; I just booked it; I had to be there.

Lou and I carried on discussing whether or not to move forward with purchasing the publishing package I'd learned about. Lou agreed that what I had to say in my book was important and could help others and that the book needed to be published in order to do that. We talked a bit about how I was receiving conflicting messages, but overall I felt that perhaps this was the best way to get published. The cost of the package was pretty high and I wanted to think about things over the next little bit and just see where I ended up.

We cleaned up after supper and went upstairs to the office with the intent of writing a bit more and also trying to see what else I could find out online that might make my decision process a bit clearer. I sat down at my desk and figured I would pull up the Twitter feed to see what was happening in Twitter world. That's when I noticed someone had tweeted Theo twice and one of the tweets was about looking forward to attending the March event in Calgary that Theo and Kim were putting on.

This naturally grabbed my attention since I was already committed to going and the event was on my radar, so to speak. When I looked to see who had posted the tweet, I was instantly more intrigued: it was Influence Publishing. My reaction was, "Hmm. Here's another publishing house that I haven't explored. Maybe I should check them out before I make any decisions about the other company."

I remember almost laughing out loud at the irony of bumping into that tweet when it seemed like I needed guidance the most. I Googled the company name and visited their website (www.influencepublishing.com). When I began to read the information on Influence's website, I became more and more excited. I felt that old familiar pull to keep on doing what I was doing. I instinctively knew I was on the right track.

I scrolled down until I came across the contact information and then I sent the company an email. I explained who I was and a little bit about the book I was writing and how I was looking for some additional information about the whole publishing process. I mentioned in the email that I had been investigating different publishers and had been in discussions with one of those publishers earlier that day. I also talked about how when I saw the tweets on Twitter via Theo Fleury, I almost laughed out loud since he has played such a significant role in the list of events I have experienced in the past year and he would be a part of my story. I also mentioned they could feel free to contact me directly if that would be easier for them.

I knew better than to think this was all just a strange coincidence. My soul spot knew better as well. I just had to figure out what the reason was.

Before too long, I received a reply from Influence Publishing; they thanked me for my email and for my interest in their company. They thought it was great that I came across them through Theo Fleury. The email went on to explain that as a publishing house they focus on books that are meant to influence positive change in the world and they are always excited to connect with authors who also want to share this message. It went on to mention that Julie Salisbury, the publisher and founder at Influence, is greatly interested in topics relating to empowerment and healing. They thought it sounded like I had a very compelling and inspirational story to share and they felt it would be great to set up a time to chat so they could hear more about my book idea. They could then fill me in on some additional services that they as a company provide to their authors.

Right away, I felt the pull of my soul spot strengthen; in fact, it was really pulling hard, so hard there was no way to ignore what it was trying to say. To me it said, "Sit up straight and pay attention, girl; this is something you need to investigate further."

Arrangements were made for me to have a discussion over the

phone with one of the ladies at Influence the next week and for me to send her a sample chapter and answer some questions that were on a worksheet she had attached to the email. Now keep in mind, at this point I was still very cautious. I had already spent an hour and a half on the phone with the rep from the other publishing company so I wasn't really holding my breath that anything would come of this phone call, but I must admit I was crossing my fingers. I let Lou know about the conversations I had been having with Influence and how I felt really pulled toward them. We agreed it was best to keep an open mind and see where this all would lead, if anywhere, before moving forward with either this new company or the old self-publishing company.

The Christmas season was upon us and I had plenty of things going on that would pass the time while I waited for the day of our scheduled phone conversation. I was having a hard time being patient about the whole situation and just wished the day would "get here already." Finally, the day arrived and I hoped that maybe I would be able to see with a bit more clarity just how I needed to proceed. The phone rang as I was preparing to head out to a restaurant not far from our office for lunch with Lou and our friend Cary. I ended up walking and talking with Gulnar, the representative from Influence Publishing, the whole way to the restaurant, as well as the entire time we waited to be taken to our seats.

I tried hard to focus on answering all the questions that the lady had and also tried to understand what she had to say at the same time. What I took away from our conversation was that Julie Salisbury was indeed interested in talking with me in person and we would have to set up a time in the new year when I could speak directly to her. I mentioned we were planning a holiday to the Dominican Republic in the first two weeks of January and that, aside from that, I would be open to whatever time worked for Julie. It was never full-on mentioned that Theo was in discussions with Influence about possibly going through them to publish his next book, but I had a bit of a sneaking suspicion of it, due to the references that were made to how my story was so intertwined with Theo's.

I got off the phone and we were now in the restaurant waiting for a table. I can remember the feeling of something electric flowing through me: it was excitement and I felt just like a little kid, almost giddy. The whole thing was not like I was offered some big book deal or anything. In fact, it wasn't that at all. It was more the thrill of actually feeling the genuine interest shown by this company and I began looking forward to whatever was coming. I had a dream and it was beginning to look like that dream might just turn into a reality, and that for me, was exhilarating!

I remember saying to Lou and Cary how funny it would be if Theo happened to be writing a book with this publisher too. How ironic! What are the chances of that? Pretty slim, I thought, but wouldn't that be a cool coincidence? And even more exciting was the chance that just maybe Theo's and my paths were set to cross, yet again. I wondered whether this could be of any significance.

My thoughts took me to my dad and to something that he quite often said to me when I was struggling with something. He would quote this most often when I was a teenager and pouting about something that hadn't gone my way and I didn't understand why. It is a quote from a poem by Max Ehrmann, called "Desiderata: A Poem for a Way of Life," and it reads:

"You are a child of the universe no less than the trees and the stars; you have a right to be here. And whether or not it is clear to you, no doubt the universe is unfolding as it should."

The line that Dad often said—and I admit at the time that he said it, I would roll my eyes and think that he was nuts—was, "And whether or not it is clear to you, no doubt the universe is unfolding as it should, Kelli, my dear; the universe is unfolding as it should."

As I grow older and wiser, I think of him quoting that quite often and I wonder, maybe my old man wasn't nuts at all. Maybe he just saw the bigger picture, the same one I see when I follow my soul spot, and I thank him for the wisdom he has given me.

So there I sat, closer than I had ever been to realizing my dream of telling my story, the closest I had ever been to feeling like I could make a difference. My soul spot was telling me that I was on track and yet I remained cautious about getting too excited too fast.

Soon enough the time arrived for Lou and me to travel to the Dominican Republic for a winter holiday with our friends Cary and Karen. We were gone for two weeks and during the last couple of days of blissful time spent lounging by the pool, I checked over my emails and there in my inbox was a message from Influence Publishing requesting a time to set up a phone conversation with Julie Salisbury. All right, I admit, I was pretty excited and hopeful that our future conversation would lead me to the goal I was seeking. I replied and we agreed that just a week following our return to the land of snow and shovelling, Julie would call me and we would have a chat.

Sure enough, as scheduled, Julie called and we spoke for quite some time. She really seemed to be genuinely interested and threw out some exceptional ideas for marketing. She encouraged me also to think about what I would like to see happen once the book is published. Did I want to start a business based on helping other survivors or did I want to speak to groups of teens, government agencies?

She was really coming up with some great ideas I hadn't considered before. Right there I felt better about not being just a faceless client who would pad the company's bank account. She talked a bit about Theo and Kim and how she would be meeting with the two of them the following week to discuss possibly working together. We both agreed that the timing of all this was incredible, if it all worked out. She was thrilled that my book had so much content about the things I had experienced with Theo and Little Warriors over the past several months.

She wondered if perhaps I would be willing to travel to Vancouver the following month so we could sit down together, figure out the direction my book would take, and see if we would be a good fit for each other as far as publishing goes. It would also be a good opportunity for me to attend one of her workshops, which would help me figure out the direction I want my book to take.

She suggested something I hadn't thought of at all in my previous writing; it took me off guard, but it really made sense. When I told her how my book started with stories of back to when I was a child, she suggested I not include those in my book, but rather provide a snapshot of the last several months since attending the Victor Walk and talk about what each of those events has meant to me.

In other words, she wanted me to talk about my survival and finding my voice and not about the abuse itself. Her reasoning was that if I were hoping to reach other people who had been abused and to encourage them to find their voices, I would have better luck doing that if they didn't have to worry about my story possibly triggering them to return to their own painful past.

I thought about that and at first was a little hesitant. But once I thought about myself personally, I realized that even I have a hard time reading stories that contain the details of abuse toward a child. I had never really thought of that before, but when I looked at my bookshelf, I could see that it was sprinkled with that type of book, which, I am sad to say, I was never able to read. She suggested that I consider all my previous writing to be part of the process that I needed to go through in order to heal. She suggested I keep the old writing, but not include it in this book. I agreed to do that and really began looking forward to the process of getting this past year down on paper.

I agreed travel to Vancouver to meet with her and attend her workshop where I would connect with other authors. I hung up the phone and immediately felt exhilarated! This company actually gave a shit about the story and about me as well. I had felt the connection in my soul spot immediately and, as you know, I just don't mess with that!

As the days passed and the time drew nearer to heading to Vancouver, Lou and I talked more and more about this new opportunity. Lou agreed that everything sounded very promising; however, he was looking for reassurance about who this publishing company was. The contract was going to mean a large financial commitment on our part, as well as on the publisher's, and Lou thought it might be best to ask Theo what his thoughts were and whether I could feel good about working with this company.

I understood Lou's unease, since he was not the one who had spoken to them over the phone and he really just wanted someone else to say, "Yes, they are a good company and they won't just run off with your money."

So there I was again messaging Theo and asking his opinion on whether or not he felt good about this company and Julie the publisher. He responded with a simple, "Yes, she's great," and that was all Lou and I needed to feel good about moving forward. I felt silly asking Theo, but I didn't know anyone else who might have had experience with Influence. Lou's thoughts were that anyone could say they were in talks with Theo and Kim and we would be unable to confirm that, other than by asking Theo ourselves. Once that confirmation came, I began to really feel excited. I could see this was a real opportunity and so could Lou.

My son Tony had just moved to Vancouver a month prior to my planned trip date and was staying with my brother Joe, so I was also really happy to be able to see him and get a small taste of the world he was working so hard at making his own. Once again, I was left amazed at how everything seemed to be coming together. There was just too much coincidence for any of it to actually be a coincidence. The universe was undoubtedly unfolding as it should.

THE TAKEAWAY LESSON

Trust in yourself and never be afraid to follow your gut. It often sees what the mind cannot.

Chapter Twelve

Dream to Reality

At last, the day to travel to Vancouver had arrived. I was a little nervous about travelling by myself on the plane, even though I had flown alone a number of times when I was in my late twenties, working for a consultant. I worried that I might miss my connecting flight and then I worried about finding the right gate and, once I was finally aboard the flight from Calgary to Vancouver, I worried that I wouldn't be able to find the baggage claim area.

Normally, I wouldn't have worried at all about those things. It is not typical of my personality to stew over things like that so I couldn't help but wonder if perhaps what I was feeling was simply excitement and what I was actually nervous about was my meeting with Julie and attending the workshop.

As soon as my plane landed, I began to feel a bubble of anticipation rising up in my stomach toward my chest. This could very well be the start of a new life for me and definitely, it was a step in the right direction toward helping other people. As I waited for my brother Joe and my son Tony to pick me up at the arrivals area, I marvelled at how wonderfully mild the weather was compared to Lethbridge. I loved the fact that rain was falling in February and the grass was already green.

I could taste the saltiness of the ocean on my lips and felt that same familiar pull toward the coast that I feel every time I am on Canada's west coast. Even though I have never lived on the coast I have always felt as though I am coming home when I visit and I hate to leave. I have a mental argument with myself about how living there is not an option at this point in my life and then I promise myself that, should my family and children decide to move away from Lethbridge, I will drag Lou to the coast even if he is kicking and screaming all the way. The pull of the ocean on my soul spot is very real and also very hard to ignore, especially since I pay such close attention to what my soul spot tells me. Who knows? Life has a funny way of falling into place when the universe does its unfolding-as-it-should thing.

The other person who has felt incredibly pulled to life on the coast is my son Tony, who with commendable courage, has followed his calling and moved to Vancouver. He was extremely excited to share with me some of the new things he had experienced in the month since he had moved. One of Tony's must-do items while I was visiting was to ride the skytrain downtown. Since my workshop the following day was to take place in Gastown, a quaint district within Vancouver's downtown core, I agreed to take the skytrain downtown right away and we could then see where my meetings would take place in the morning. We walked the wet streets of downtown and I listened as he shared some of his experiences and favourite findings of the past month.

When we approached the building where the workshop would take place, I couldn't help but feel pulled toward one of the shops along the street. It was getting to be pretty late and most of the storefronts were closed with the exception of a few coffee houses, bars, and restaurants. Still, the dimmed lights of one of the shops beckoned me to take note. I commented to Tony that I would need to take a peek inside that shop at some point before I left Vancouver; I wasn't sure exactly why, but there must be a reason for it.

Having found our destination for the weekend workshop, and now feeling confident we would be able to find it without too much trouble the following day, we continued on. After stopping for a quick bite to eat, we made our way back to the skytrain and to my brother's apartment.

The anticipation for the workshop was almost too much to handle. Sleep finally came, but not before I had spent a few hours lying awake and mulling over the possibilities rolling through my mind. I struggled through the feelings of self-doubt and reminded myself there was a reason I was there attending this workshop. I needed to stop resisting and let life flow the way it needs to.

I allowed myself to dream of the possibilities that could come. What if all this were much bigger than the book itself? What if it leads to a career focused on helping others to heal? My silent dreams of a life filled with helping others heal could be on the verge of becoming a reality. I knew I was ready for whatever challenges might lie ahead; I had prepared my whole life for this opportunity and it was time for me to begin to take action. I silenced my inner critic and eventually drifted off to sleep with visions of myself speaking to a large group of people floating through my head.

Thoughts of the day that lay ahead danced through my mind, while I jumped out of bed and made my way to Joe's kitchen to make a coffee. What would this day hold? Am I ready for this? How long will it take to drive downtown? How many deep cleansing breaths can one take? Why have the butterflies in my tummy turned into great big bats? What if they don't like me? What if they hate my story? Could this be the start of something great? Why does it have to be raining today? My hair will be a ball of frizz.

On and on my thoughts raced, along with all the emotions attached. My mind was so consumed with them that I hardly remember the drive to Gastown. Once inside the building, much to my amazement, the voices in my head settled and I resigned myself to allow this process to take place in whatever way it needed to. Letting go of the underlying urge to control its outcome provided me with the peace of mind I needed. Whatever happened would be because that was the way things needed to happen.

Alina, a communications and administrative assistant at Influence, met us at the door and led us up to the office where we would be spending the next two days. There were seven other authors taking part in the weekend workshop with me and they trickled in shortly after I arrived. The space that we occupied had a very soothing décor. Our seats were arranged around a large boardroom-style table in the centre. The ledges around the room were filled with books that Influence had published, providing us with visual teasers of what the future would hold should we decide to publish our stories. None of us really knew what to expect; the room was filled with the energy that comes with quiet anticipation.

The moment Julie walked in the room she seemed to calm us all with her welcoming and friendly demeanour; it was exactly what we needed. She led us through a series of activities all designed to help us through the enormous process of bringing our books from the dream stage to the final publishing stage and the marketing that would follow.

We began by answering a number of carefully selected questions about our stories and who our target market would be and why. We described what our readers could expect to gain by reading our books. I was absolutely tickled with the wide variety of books that were being worked on. Each of us had quite different stories to tell, ranging from business success to a complex fantasy novel and everything in between. I found it inspiring to hear each person talk about what the motivation behind their book was; it was uplifting to hear all the words of encouragement offered to each other throughout the day.

The entire first day was totally packed with activities and discussions, each of them providing unexpected insights, which all of us very much needed as we began our journeys to becoming published authors. At the end of the day, Julie gave us our evening homework assignment and we each went our own way, some of us overwhelmed, some of us exhausted, and all of us inspired.

As I waited for Tony and Joe to pick me up in front of the building, I found myself standing in front of the display to the shop I had felt pulled toward the evening before. I tried to resist its pull again, since I did not want to go in and have Tony and Joe wonder and worry where I was. I turned and looked in the display window to try and see what was pulling at me. I spotted a small wooden box tucked away in the back of the display case and it had what appeared to be some sort of frog carved into the lid. Try to resist as I did, it was no use. I had to go into the shop. It pulled me in like a magnet to metal and there was nothing I could do but allow it.

I quickly popped into the shop for a closer look at the box I had spotted in the window. In fact, a frog was carved into the lid, but the frog reminded me of something you would see if you were on hallucinogens: it was stretched and had a really sad look on its face. That was not what I was hoping for. Just as I turned to leave, I caught a glimpse of another frog carving mounted by a stick onto a small block of wood. The frog had an aboriginal feel to it, and parts of it were painted yellow, black, red, and green. Aha! Yes, this was it; this is what was pulling me! The frog had a striking resemblance to the Victor frog that is tattooed on my forearm.

Without further hesitation, I picked up the frog and paid for it, sharing my excitement with the storeowner. When I showed him my tattoo, he agreed that this piece of art I had just purchased seemed like a perfect fit. I turned to leave, but again just as before, I was pulled in the direction of a jewellery showcase that appeared to contain a collection of silver earrings, necklaces, and rings. Well, holy crap, I kid you not, there was a small delicate hand-carved silver frog pendant, also bearing a striking resemblance to my Victor tattoo. I quickly pointed out my find to the shopkeeper and had him ring that purchase in as well. He put the new necklace in a pretty little box with a small bow on it because, as he said, this was a very special gift to myself and it deserved a very special box.

I thanked the fellow and returned to my spot outside just in time for Tony and Joe to pick me up.

I could hardly believe that the small shop I had been so pulled to enter contained one of my most important symbols on this journey. There I was, taking one more step to heal myself and help others heal, and I couldn't think of anything more fitting to remind myself of that.

The ride back to my brother's house was a blur; I actually have no real memory of it at all. The only thing that remains imprinted on my mind are the feelings of awe over how this trip was all unfolding so perfectly. I felt like I was exactly where I needed to be and I was totally content with that.

Once we arrived at the house, I sat down to begin my home-work assignment for the evening but, try as I might, my brain was reduced to working like a mass of melted marshmallow; I was emotionally drained. I needed to give it a rest.

Tony and I walked around the neighbourhood and I listened as he pointed out all the new places he had discovered. He listened to me babble on about how exciting my day had been. He sure was a great sounding board for all my thoughts and I treasured each and every moment with him, knowing it could be quite some time before we would be able to be together again. During our walk, I couldn't help but feel so proud of my son for having the courage to step out of his comfort zone and go after the dream he had been mulling over for the past three years. Here he was, nineteen-years old and he had transplanted himself into a large city—no job, no friends, and no safety net—just a dream for something better. Perhaps that is what made him such a great confidant for me: he too had felt the fear and insecurities of the unknown and had taken a deep breath and made a commitment to live his dreams the best way he could. In the face of it all, he had taken the time to encourage me to do the same, to embrace the fear of change, knowing I will make a difference to someone else.

Feeling refreshed from our walk, I sat down once again and was able to piece together my assignment, although I was not totally happy with it. I felt I could ask the others for input in the morning. That was the beauty of this workshop: we had immediate access to very constructive and personal feedback from a variety of different personalities.

I packed up my assignment in the portfolio-type black zipper binder that was given to each author to help us organize our writings and flopped onto the bed feeling utterly exhausted, emotionally drained, and very much looking forward to the workshop the next morning. As tired as I was, my sleep was restless: my mind wouldn't stop racing. Thoughts about the events of my day passed through my head right alongside my dreams for the future and my curious wonder about how the next day would go.

Bright and early that Sunday morning, Tony and I set off for the skytrain that would take us to downtown Vancouver. I was still feeling unsure of exactly how to get where I needed to go, so it was a relief to have Tony offer to be my escort. We arrived downtown and set out to grab a coffee and a quick bite to eat before heading to Gastown for my workshop.

Rain had begun to turn into snow and it was slowly starting to stick to the ground, which as Joe informed me was a recipe for disaster in a city that rarely had to deal with much more than rain. I guess it was lucky for us that we took transit downtown, and the worst that we had to deal with was slush and soaking wet socks and shoes.

I was too excited about what lay ahead of me at the workshop to care much about my sopping wet feet; they would dry soon enough, but probably just in time for me to head out and get them all wet again on the way home. Throughout it all, I was certain I was exactly where I needed to be, doing exactly what I needed to do, for myself and other Victors as well. So, a little lacking in solid sleep but overflowing with enthusiasm, I headed into the building for what promised to be another interesting day in the workshop.

When I walked in, the calm surroundings and the welcoming

people instantly put me at ease. I think that for the first time ever I felt like I was an author and I could see everything coming together, one piece and one step at a time. I was relieved to see that the other participants had also struggled with the evening's homework. We all questioned if what we had written was what we were actually supposed to have written, and it was great to see that we really were much more on track than we had given ourselves credit for. Before too long, we had each determined what the title, subtitle, and synopsis were for our books. For the most part, they were all quite different than what we had envisioned them to be when we began the process.

Our workshop reminded me that I have had experience in the past with the process of collective, creative brainstorming. Each person offered input into each other's work as we went along if the urge hit us. What resulted was a whole lot of positive and constructive feedback that helped us solidify what we were writing about and why we were writing about it.

When we dug deeper into each other's stories, we uncovered several tidbits of information that we did not recognize about ourselves. For example, one of the authors had experienced something that was beyond what anyone would call a test to their physical and emotional health, and yet she had minimized it in her story. We actually had to point out the enormity of strength and courage it had taken her to get past that obstacle before she recognized how truly amazing it was that she had got through it while running a business and a household with small children.

As I sat there and took part in that discussion, it became clear to me for the first time that the way she had gotten through that rough patch was exactly how I had survived my childhood and every major difficulty in my life as an adult. We both had made a subconscious decision to focus on what had to be done rather than the enormity of the situations we were in. It was like we had both looked at our situations and said, "There's too much that needs to be done and I just don't have time for focusing on that shit!"

It was the method we had subconsciously devised in order to survive the ordeals. What happened as a result was that neither of us had ever acknowledged the emotional pain we were going through at that time; instead we just put it all away in a box up on the top shelf to collect dust until we were ready to deal with it.

This past year has been the year that I have taken my box down off that shelf, blown off the dust, and slowly begun to investigate its contents. There has been so much about myself that I have learned, so many answers given, and so many emotions that have surfaced. By looking at the contents of my box, I have been able to examine all the memories inside and shred the shame attached to each one of them.

I am just beginning this healing journey and yet I have come so far and feel so much better already. Fuelled with the encouragement from my new workshop friends and from Julie, my determination has multiplied to such a level that it refuses to be ignored any longer. At long last, I am ready, so let's do this shit!

Monday came quickly, and Tony, my trusty chaperone and tour guide, came with me to North Vancouver to sign my publishing contract with Influence. We took a sea bus over to North Vancouver. Neither of us had been on one before so it was pretty cool to share in that new adventure together. We arrived at the office and began to discuss all the details we needed to address in order for the book to launch in mid-October 2014. As we were already nearing the end of February, the list of things to do seemed quite daunting.

Julie suggested that in order to meet our deadlines I would need to be working full time on completing the book. Could I be ready? How could I not be? I had come so far and so many things had fallen almost magically into place that to do otherwise just wasn't an option. I was ready to do whatever it would take to move forward. I don't want to tread water in one place or move backwards. Moving forward, just like Victor the frog, is my only acceptable option. A very small part of me wondered how Lou would feel about this, but a bigger part already knew he would have my back.

Meeting with Julie at her office and going over the contract details took longer than I had expected. I had a plane to catch in only a few hours. Julie and I made plans to work on the book a bit more when we would meet up at Theo and Kim's forum on March 14 in Calgary.

Tony and I were pretty much running to catch our skytrain back to Joe's neighbourhood. We managed to squeeze in among the commuters who were making their way out of the downtown core at rush hour. I was overflowing with gratitude and excitement about the success of the weekend and the future that lay ahead. I didn't care that everyone on the transit system was quiet, barely even making eye contact with each other. I couldn't contain my excitement, and Tony and I just carried out our conversation as if we were the only two people on the train.

I managed to text Lou to let him know I had signed the contract and that I would need to be working full time at the book in order to meet my deadlines. Shortly after that, Tony and I were practically running through the ever-increasing level of slush to get back to Joe's in time for me to meet my plane. Our umbrellas proved to be useless against the wetness of the sleet that was falling, since we were moving so fast, and I kept feeling like Mary Poppins who might float off with her umbrella at any moment. We decided to close the umbrellas and give in to the wetness; neither of us are sugar cubes, so we were in no danger of melting. To be honest, I was hardly aware of my soaking wet feet and how cold I was.

I had been totally focused on my discussion with Tony and our race to get back to Joe's. Poor Lou had responded to my text much earlier but I had not heard my phone notify me, and our current pace would have made responding almost impossible even if I had. As it turned out, we were in such a rush to get to the airport that I didn't respond until much later and, by the time

I did, I realized there was just too much to talk about over text messages or a phone call. Our discussion would have to wait.

I arrived back in Lethbridge at around 12:30 in the morning and my excitement had given way to total exhaustion. Lou was awake when I got home and we were finally able to discuss my adventures and what it meant to our real estate business. I held my breath and waited for an objection. What I got instead was congratulations and total support. His last words before he went to sleep were, "I'm so lucky to be sleeping with an author."

And with a smile on my face and a happy heart, I drifted off to sleep.

The following couple of weeks leading up to Theo and Kim's forum in Calgary were spent writing in our office at home. I kept waiting for Lou to get frustrated, but day after day the only thing that happened was an increase in his encouragement. Since I had been totally committed to writing, Lou had taken over my clients and calls, and allowed me to focus completely on the task at hand.

In fact, often when I would offer to put lunch or supper together for us, he would tell me he would take care of it and to just keep writing. When I thanked him for all his help one day, he responded by telling me that his role in this was to make sure my life was as stress-free as possible so I could do what I needed to do. It thrilled me to hear him tell people about what I was doing and why I was doing it. He was so proud of me and was quickly becoming my biggest cheerleader. I am so blessed to have him in my life and I know for a fact that without his continued support I would not be able to do this.

We had discussed the possibilities of what may lie ahead once the book gets published and we both agree that the book is just the beginning. I owe it to myself to seek out opportunities that can get me in front of more people and spread the message of hope. So few people actually find what they are passionate about and even fewer can align that with their careers. I'm not sure where this can lead; but I can tell you I will be ready to go wherever that is, once it becomes apparent.

During my time writing this book, I have been plagued with feelings of self-doubt. I continually had to reassure myself that I am just the storyteller who is trying to inspire others to find their voices; the editor would help to make sure that it is done in a way that would make people want to read it.

In the days leading up to my planned trip to Calgary, I continued to receive messages from friends and acquaintances thanking me for what I was doing. Some disclosed their own abuse and I was very surprised how many of them had never told a soul before telling me. I can only imagine the relief they must have felt, finally being able to confide in somebody. And I felt absolutely honoured that they had chosen that somebody to be me. I had inspired them and they in turn had inspired me. This is what it is all about and the messages they sent me were all the fuel I would need to keep myself forging ahead. You all know who you are and I really just want to make sure you know how much your courage has helped me, and that because of the encouragement you gave, I have been able to make this dream into a reality; so really, together we have helped others!

THE TAKEAWAY LESSON

Sometimes the biggest difference that you will make is in the lives of others. When people can see you courageously trying to improve, it also inspires them to see what they are capable of. Never stop trying.

Chapter Thirteen

Conversations In Healing

I am standing in the Calgary International Airport, feeling excited about seeing Julie again, and very much looking forward to participating in Theo and Kim's forum tomorrow. I can't help but notice how I have been feeling like I am waiting for a friend rather than waiting for my publisher. Somehow, we have connected and even though I have only spent a couple of days with Julie, it feels as though we have known each other for years.

She walked through the arrival doors and I felt a jolt of excitement run through me. In picking her up, I felt as though I was retrieving a puzzle piece that was needed in order to carry on with the upcoming events. We were immediately comfortable with each other and quickly our conversation filled with the sharing of significant events that have happened in the couple of weeks since we last saw each other. There were no awkward pauses, no uncomfortable feelings of unease; we simply picked up where we left off and it became clear to me that I had in fact made the right choice in deciding to work with Influence Publishing.

Together, we enjoyed each other's company and conversation throughout the evening, until at last it was time for sleep and we drifted off, each of us very much looking forward to attending the forum in the morning.

The much-too-soft mattresses along with our racing thoughts about the upcoming events played their part in making sure we were both awake prior to our alarms going off. Julie had some background work that needed to be done for the forum and I had planned on meeting up with Heather and Torre who were also registered for the event.

At last, everyone was together and it was time to take our seats. We all anxiously awaited the start of the day's program. We had no expectations as to what we were in for.

I felt a gentle hand on my shoulder and turned to find Becky smiling down at me. I hadn't seen her since the Little Warriors' press release in Calgary for their new ad campaign in the summer and yet, even after only connecting that once before, I felt the joy of seeing an old friend. We greeted each other with a huge hug and I felt so grateful for the connections I have made along the way this year. How incredible that our bond together moved us from relative strangers to feeling like old friends through this journey. I felt as though she and I are connected in the strongest, most silent way, and it feels great! It doesn't matter that I don't know her history or her family or what makes her laugh and cry. What matters is we are two people trying to make the world a better place and there is an unspoken understanding that this is the start of a very long friendship. Strange how sometimes you just know.

Julie took the stage, welcomed all of us, and introduced members of Theo and Kim's families, along with special counsellors who were on hand in case any of us found we needed support through a particular subject or if we were to find ourselves triggered in any way by the discussions. Julie explained that the day would be separated into three parts. In the first portion, Theo would tell us his story and then Kim would provide us with information on the trauma of child sexual abuse and the effects it has on the brain and how we learn the ability to soothe ourselves when we experience it from infancy onward. She would also highlight parts of Theo's story and how they relate to trauma. After that, Kim and Theo would conduct an impromptu therapy session together and lastly, we as an audience would be invited to join in the discussion with any comments or questions we might have.

Theo began his story. It was one I have heard before and also read about. The difference on that day was that he spent a bit more time discussing the obstacles that his parents faced in their lives that ultimately rendered them unable to be more present in his life. I love that when Theo talked about this, he spoke without blame; only with understanding and acceptance. He realized his parents were only doing the best they could with the circumstances they had. I could feel through what he was saying and how he was saying it that approaching the problem that way had helped him avoid what most likely could have been a natural reaction of blaming or resenting them both.

Theo concluded his talk by encouraging all of us to find our voices. He talked about how many people have shared their stories with him along his journey and that, even though he is only one person, he has made a huge impact on the face of releasing the shame and trauma of child sexual abuse. He asked us to imagine what the outcome would be if he had help, if we all spoke up. He spoke about the Victor Walk and even mentioned that Heather, Kim, Becky, and I had all been there with him. It felt really good to know we had made a difference to him by being there. Sometimes, I think we forget that he also needs the community of Victors and is probably relieved with the amount of support that he has received.

It all starts with the first step we take toward shredding the shame. And what happens beyond that? Well, that is truly a miracle.

We had a fifteen-minute break and then Kim began the process of explaining about trauma, what can cause it, and what some of the typical affects are. I listened quietly and found myself very intrigued by what she was saying. Most of her presentation served as a confirmation to what I already knew to some degree. But then, she started discussing the cycle of abuse and trauma, and how it could be generational. She told us that when a caregiver—be it a mom or a dad or another parental figure— struggles with their own issues and is emotionally detached and unable to soothe their children, the children will then themselves experience trauma.

Theo, for example, referred to having a constant feeling of

anxiety except when he was playing hockey. Hockey for him was soothing; it was a distraction from the emotional turmoil he was trying to cope with. The first time he experienced a calming of that turmoil was when he had his first drink and, as a result, he kept right on drinking, enjoying the peace that came with it for probably the first time in his life. The anxiety and emotional turmoil did not disappear, but rather it was numbed to a tolerable level.

Kim also discussed triggers and how sometimes things in the world around us—be they smells, sounds, conversations, or any number of things—will trigger us to respond as if we are in danger or experiencing actual trauma. One of the ways I really related to this is the way I zone out mentally. That is really one of the biggest aftereffects I feel. Kim talked about how these periods of zoning out can happen when we as adults are trying unsuccessfully to parent our own children and our children inadvertently become victims of trauma, because of our inability to soothe them.

I looked at Torre and she looked at me; we exchanged glances that we both knew meant—shit! Our poor kids! I thought back to my first marriage when my two children were quite small. I had spent days being checked out mentally, and as a result those two little guys were forced to figure out how to soothe themselves. I had finally managed to break free from a very unhealthy spousal relationship, but I was unable to get full custody of my kids; they were forced to spend one week with me and one week with their dad. I tried very hard, but in the end the system that was supposed to protect them, actually ended up failing them, and they were forced to remain trapped in an abusive situation.

I immediately text messaged Ali, my daughter, and told her that I couldn't wait to get home to see her—I had so much to share with her and I apologized for not being there to protect her as a little girl. Her response was to tell me she loves me and that it wasn't my fault; she knew I had done the best I could. I am so thankful that both my kids are so loving and that they know how much I love them.

I listened as Kim talked, and I thought about how badly my children and I need trauma therapy. We need to begin to repair ourselves from the damage caused so long ago; time to put down the bags of emotional crap we've carried.

Hearing Kim discuss trauma was an eye-opening experience: on the one hand I realized I had caused trauma for my kids, the two most precious people in the world to me, by being unable to remove them from their father's abuse. And on the other hand, I understood I could only use the tools I had in my toolbox at the time and I had done the absolute best I could.

Throughout the day, great pains were taken to ensure that the environment was "safe" and that hopefully through the sharing of Theo's story and through Kim's presentation, we as an audience, would feel comfortable enough to take part in the conversations during the last portion of the forum. Kim and Theo took their places onstage in two big chairs put there for them. Watching them get comfortable, I found myself wondering just how they were going to go about this impromptu therapy session and whether it would be something rehearsed or truly off the cuff.

Theo and Kim started the session by discussing their reactions to a blog post (www.theofleury14.com/2014/03/08/compassion-for-offenders/) that had gone out only days before this forum. The blog post had sparked anger and resentment in a number of readers and as a result, both Kim and Theo had been wrestling with different emotions. I had personally read the blog and offered my comments on it, so I knew exactly which blog they were discussing. I found it very interesting to hear them talk about the different ways they had felt affected by the comments readers had posted. Kim's husband Bob Spensley had written the blog and Theo had posted it on Facebook and asked people for their thoughts on the subject.

More or less, the blog suggests that perhaps our abusers also need compassion from the angle that hurt people are the ones who hurt people. Bob acknowledges on Facebook that this is a concept in healing and that although it makes sense to him, he was unsure that he would be able to practise it in real life if someone ever hurt his daughter. The post talks about how our anger and hatred toward our abusers has an ill effect on ourselves physically and emotionally, and that the actual abuse often isn't what hurts the most, but it is rather how people, including ourselves, respond to the abuse that makes healing difficult or even relatively easy.

Bob writes that if we victims were able to see that our abuse had resulted because of someone else's issues and pains, we would be able to release the thought that the abuse was somehow our fault and instantly be able to focus our energy on healing and loving ourselves. The side effect of this train of thought is that if our abusers are able to feel less pain as a result of compassion from us victims, then they are less likely to cause further pain in others. That would help to end the cycle of abuse. Where the negative feedback came about was partially due to the fact that people misinterpreted the blog to mean we must forgive our abusers; they felt it offered an excuse for the abuser to have abused.

I did not see it that way at all, partially I suppose because from a very young age, probably nine or ten, I had often wondered what made my abuser do what he did. I know for me personally that thinking that way has helped me to understand that my abuse was not the result of anything I did; it was his issue that perhaps was a result of something being wrong with his "hard wiring," or even possibly his having experienced abuse in childhood.

It is important to note that not all pedophiles have been abused as children; however, a great number have, and while that number is high it does not in any way mean that just because someone is abused they are likely to abuse someone else. In fact, very few of us who have been abused end up being abusers.

The arguments for and against compassionate thinking are understandable; I am intrigued by the discussion on both sides. I also think the more I understand what is meant by the word "compassion" in this context and the more I look at the intention that Bob had when he wrote it, the easier it is for me to see that perhaps this is a necessary part of the healing process.

A statement was made to the audience and I was so consumed with digesting its meaning that I now can't even recall who made the statement. It basically said that if every victim of the trauma of child sexual abuse deserves the right to heal, does that not include the victims who then become abusers as well? Clarification was given. The statement in no way was meant to forgive the abuser from a standpoint of having abused; the abuse cycle is separate from the need for abusers to heal from whatever it is that causes them to become abusers. Thus, more or less, we were looking at the cycle of abuse as a problem that is much like the chicken and the egg. Which comes first? There is never any doubt or suggestion that what our abusers have done is anything less than vile and damaging, and has a catastrophic effect on its victims. The topic is simply challenging us to look at the whole cycle of abuse and how it can be stopped.

Sitting there listening to them both talk left me feeling a new level of respect for them both. While this is a touchy and also extremely difficult subject, particularly when an audience is full of victims of that kind of abuse, both Kim and Theo found the courage to have this conversation in the name of helping people to heal and end the cycle. I applaud them for that and also believe these are the types of discussions that need to take place if we are going to have a chance at ending this vicious cycle. This topic is not an easy one and I could easily debate it here for a whole chapter, but that is not the point of mentioning it.

The point is I am beginning to understand that both Theo and Kim really do care about making sure they are doing things that will help people. I can now see they are vulnerable and susceptible to feelings of insecurity, just like everyone else. This automatically had the effect of increasing my comfort level and created a "safe place" feeling for me. I wondered if the other people in the room were also feeling that way or if it would take something more to bring them out of their shells.

As the discussion went on and people began to join in the conversation, it became clear that we were not all quite feeling comfortable enough to open up just yet. Julie carried a microphone to each person who had a comment to offer or a question to ask. She made her way from person to person and then something truly incredible happened. She stopped at a table and a young boy stood up to speak. Kim asked him if he would be more comfortable sharing from his table or if he would like to go up on stage with Kim and Theo and talk from there. He decided he would like to hop up on stage to talk.

Kim and Theo brought in another chair and placed it in between them onstage. Just as confident as can be, the boy, whom I will call Ben, sat down to say what he had to say. He began, "Hi, my name is Ben and I am ten-years old and I am a survivor of child sexual abuse." The attention of everyone in the room was now totally focused on this brave young guy. Kim asked Ben who it was that he felt safe in first sharing his story with and Ben told her that it was his grandma. When Kim asked him why he thought it was that he found the courage to tell his grandma, he simply responded with, "Well, I didn't want to be touched in those places anymore."

I looked around the room at the faces of all the adults who were wrestling with speaking up themselves and I saw complete admiration. Kim asked Theo what he thought about Ben and his story and Theo said, "Well, I think I have a new hero!" Everyone in the room stood up and gave Ben a well-deserved round of applause. I could feel myself begin to well over with emotion; tears of admiration had pooled up in my eyes and were making their way down my cheeks. The look of pride and happiness on

Ben's face was just awesome. The entire atmosphere of the room changed instantly. People stood up to thank Ben for his courage and to show him how much they admired his ability to do what so many of us had not yet felt strong enough to do.

Ben showed us, by his matter-of-fact approach to sharing his story, that he did not feel any shame. And why should he? After all, it was nothing that he should feel ashamed about. I could see others were realizing that if Ben could do this, so could they. One by one, audience members began to stand up and find their voices. I can't help but think about this book and feel encouraged by just how much of an impact one person's courage has on the lives of others.

My thoughts go back once again to the Victor Walk, the start of it all for me. Theo's story and the stories shared by others who have found the courage to share started a ripple in the ocean that will continue to grow in size, gaining momentum to become the equivalent of a tidal wave that will wash away the shame that is felt by millions.

Now that people in the audience had grabbed onto the inspiration provided by Ben, people who wanted to contribute were raising their hands all over the room. Julie took the microphone to everyone who wanted to speak, until Kim noticed a shift in the room's energy and suggested it was unlikely much more healing could occur effectively with low energy. The next comment would be the final one to conclude the day.

I listened as Kim talked about therapy being much like a conversation and how even being able to talk with friends or loved ones can be therapeutic. Memories floated through my mind of conversations that I have been a part of that have helped me or someone else through tough times. I thought about all the people who haven't told anyone about their abuse and how much relief they would feel if they were only able to talk about it.

I hoped that people left there that day feeling encouraged to have those much-needed healing conversations. Julie brought the microphone over to an audience member who then shared her comments in a way that brought the event to a natural close. The forum ended and as I walked out of the room I glanced back to see if I could get a glimpse of the shame being left behind. I could not see it with my eyes, but I could feel it in my heart. Many of the people who had attended the forum that day walked out with renewed hope and inspiration, minus the heavy burden of shame they had been carrying for so many years.

I can't believe how emotionally spent and physically tired I was feeling following this event. It was only 4:30 p.m. and there was still a full evening ahead before I would be able to close my eyes and feel the soothing embrace of much-needed sleep. Julie invited me to join her, Theo, and Kim along with the other members of the group who had helped make the forum possible, for a debriefing over dinner. I felt somewhat awkward and I worried that she was only asking me because she didn't want to appear to ditch me alone in our room while she joined the others. I was prepared to go for a bite to eat with Torre before she headed back home to Lethbridge and I told Julie that so she wouldn't worry about me. Julie corrected my misjudgment of her intentions by telling me that the group valued my input and views of how I felt the forum had gone and if I thought anything needed improvement and that was why I had been invited.

As unexpected as the invitation was, it was also very welcome. I accepted the invitation telling Torre we would need to catch up once I got back to Lethbridge. Then I caught up to Julie, very much anticipating the rest of the evening. The group walked to a restaurant only a few doors down from the hotel where we were staying and we made our way to a private room tucked away in the back. It was clear that everyone was emotionally spent, but they pushed onward so that the debriefing could occur while the thoughts, suggestions, and memories from the day were still fresh and at the top of everyone's minds.

I was intrigued by the conversations around me and quite taken aback by the genuine concern that everyone had in making sure that this forum and future forums deliver positive experiences to the audience. I contributed where I could and felt thankful that I had been given the opportunity to do so. The whole experience was rather surreal to me and yet at the same time it served to show me once again that everyone is capable of making a difference to others. It reminded me that every single person in that room started out by saying they had a desire to help others and then took the first step to making that a reality.

It was not fame that brought about this forum; it was a burning desire to make a difference in people's lives, and a desire to end the cycle of abuse. I sat and thought to myself how neat it would be to attend the next forum, to witness the changes that would be made to the way some things would be done as a direct result of the conversations that we had around that dinner table.

With everyone's hunger more than satisfied, and the debriefing of events complete, I think everyone felt like they could collapse right there at the table. The day wrapped up with everyone posing for a group photo and I managed to get one for myself on my phone. I have added it to my ever-growing collection of photos I have taken this year; they provide me with encouragement to keep moving forward in my dream to help others.

As the group broke up, I turned and said goodbye to Theo and thanked him for such an incredible experience. He offered a big hug and right in the middle of it he pulled away with his hands on my shoulders and, with an unexpected burst of excitement, he asked how my book was coming and when it would be released.

There was such a shift in his energy that it made me wonder if he handled stress the same way I do, by zoning out. We'd had a few different opportunities where we could have discussed the book throughout the day, but he was noticeably distant, almost appearing as if he was completely focused on the task at hand, which in this case was the forum, before he could think about anything else. I can only imagine the pressure that he had been feeling about delivering a forum that would be beneficial to its participants. In my opinion, the forum was a complete success; I learned something new and at the same time felt the community of Victors grow even larger.

I had been so wrapped up in all the days' activities and had not really been alone up until that point. I really felt bad for not giving Lou a quick call earlier, but it seemed that a text message here and there could convey the same amount of information I was able to give him while in a group of people anyway. I called him then. I hadn't considered that Lou would be anxious to hear from me, which was rather silly given that with me gone, all he had to think about was work and what I was up to. He had been my biggest cheerleader throughout this journey; he is my rock.

Hearing the sadness in his voice over the phone at the fact that I hadn't called earlier brought me to a new realization. It made me aware that I was not on this journey alone; I need to make sure from that point on, that even if I travelled alone I should not forget the fact that he needed to feel a part of it all.

I tend to assume that people around me know how much they mean to me. I spend so much time talking about them to other people that I forget to actually let them know too. Naturally, my intention was anything but to have Lou feel out of the loop and I treasure all the support he has given me. Once again, I was reminded that one person's journey to healing involves not only themselves, but also their families and loved ones as well.

It is understandable to me that when a person such as myself goes through this self-awareness process and begins the process of healing, they tend to get wrapped up in focusing on that and may inadvertently ignore their biggest supporters. Maybe "ignore" is a harsh word; it implies that there is a conscious decision to pay less attention to someone and I don't think that is the case; not for my situation and me anyway.

The people who are in our inner circles—our friends and families—are used to us behaving in a way that has us focusing our attention on them. When we are in new relationships, we make a point of doing little things for our partners. Then at some point, we have our careers and children to focus energy on. We simply are not used to giving that same level of attention to ourselves.

There can be any number of reasons for this, but possibly because we are avoiding our negative pasts and in order to focus on who we are, it becomes nearly impossible to do that without having a good hard look at what made us who we are. Often as we get older and more secure in our careers and our families grow, our children move out and start their own paths in life. What we are left with is a bunch of extra time to look inward at who we are and what we have been through and how to begin to fix what we see as wrong or what is causing us distress.

This new self-awareness or self-discovery process is often something we haven't done before. Often the manuals and guidelines on how to do that effectively are not something we seek out in the beginning stages of our healing, and so we sometimes stumble and fall along the way. Over the years, I have read a number of books about self-awareness, but never linked them to what I was dealing with as a result of my abuse as a child. I know that Lou supports me, but there is also that element of the unknown where he wonders what will happen if, in discovering myself and what I want out of life, I discover I don't want him with me. What if I leave him behind? To me that thought doesn't even enter my mind, because I can't imagine ever wanting to walk through this journey without him by my side. I don't even think about him needing reassurance that the new confident and self-aware version of myself will definitely want him to continue along beside me. So when I was away and sidetracked, I didn't think it meant anything other than, well, I was sidetracked. I hadn't considered that from Lou's perspective I was off on another surreal adventure in my journey, while he was stuck at home holding down the fort and doing the same things he always does; I hadn't considered that just maybe he had spent the time I was away worrying that I would forget about him and leave him behind.

Change is change, whether it is for good or bad, it is still a change, and inevitably change leaves us all feeling a little unsure and uneasy. At last, it was time for the drive back home to Lethbridge. The sun was shining and I could see for miles. When I thought back to the events of this last year, all that came to mind were the words "unbelievable" and "surreal." As I looked out to the mountains in the distance, I repeated those two words over and over, and my heart filled with complete and utter gratitude for every second of it and every ounce of support given to me not only by Lou, but by my family as well. I could hardly wait to get home and spend a quiet night with my man. I know that is all he needs and I can't think of anything I would rather be doing.

THE TAKEAWAY LESSON

Every person can only do the best they can with the tools available to them at that time. Never judge yourself harshly for what you feel you could have done differently. No one wakes up in the morning wondering how he or she can screw things up that day. Each one of us wants to do the best we can for ourselves and others.

I DID

I was finally home from my few days away in Calgary and as I unloaded my luggage and turned the key to our house, I found myself feeling bummed that Lou wouldn't be home for another hour, because he would be sitting at his open houses. I was tired and in light of my oversight of not calling Lou the night before, what I really needed was to be able to give him the biggest hug and tell him how much he means to me.

The house was empty and as I walked into the kitchen, I was greeted instead by a big bouquet of beautiful pink roses that had been placed in a vase of water on the kitchen table. It was Lou's way of saying, "I love you and I missed you and I'm so glad you're home."

Tears of gratitude filled my eyes as my heart swelled with love for him. Through all my ups and downs and insecurities, he had been there and I couldn't imagine taking this journey without him by my side. Again, I wondered if everything that I had gone through as a child and young adult was put before me so that I could truly appreciate every small detail of my incredible life today. In a life riddled with hardships, there was also love, happiness, and beauty, and the worst was most definitely behind me. I had experienced so many things that I wanted to share with the people who I knew would be interested.

While I waited for Lou to get home I called my mom and gave her every little detail that I could about the events of the last few days, all the while wishing that she were back from her trip to Arizona. When I looked back to where this had all started, it occurred to me that it was about the same time the previous year that we had been discussing the need for action and wondering just how we would be able to get involved to help others. Now, one year later, so much has happened and there is clearly so much more yet to come.

The reason, in my mind for having all these new opportunities and experiences can be explained by one simple word: "Action." We all have desires, dreams, and goals, but in order for anything to change beyond what we already have, we need to make a move, take action, and be willing to fully participate in our destinies.

Colin Harms, a colleague and friend of Lou's and mine, had sat down with me over coffee shortly after the Victor Walk that began this journey ten months ago in May 2013. He had been interested in hearing about my recent adventure and a little bit more about how I became involved in it and why it was I felt I needed to go.

While we conversed over coffee, he talked about a company he was starting and I believe that the story behind why he wanted to start the company, as well as what the company is all about, ran parallel to what it is I am trying to say here.

Colin had been travelling to Scottsdale, Arizona in 2008 with a group of investors to explore a real estate acquisition opportunity. In flight, he could hear two men across the aisle from him getting excited. He listened closely as they talked about how they were planning to take part in "The Dream Car Tour." He was intrigued since these two men were around thirty-years old, well-dressed, well-spoken, and seemed to be full of life and vigour. He felt a need to be part of their conversation, so he leaned over and said, "Hey guys, that sounds really cool. Would you mind telling me more?"

Without hesitation, in sync with each other, they began telling him how they and four of their clients go to New York City and rent exotic cars for a six-day trip through the mountains. Each day, they switch cars until each has had a full day handling a Ferrari, Lamborghini, Bentley, Porsche, Aston Martin, and one other luxury vehicle. Colin's mind was racing; finally he had to ask the dreaded question. What is it that you guys do? The response came quickly and smoothly.

"Whatever we say we are going to do. We are doers!"

Colin was thinking, enough said! He leaned back in his seat and began note taking. The next hour flew by and he had come up with a statement to define his future. It went like this, "From this day on, I will act on my intuition. I will not be the person who procrastinates and continues to say, 'I wish I would have, I wish I could have, if I had gone there or if I had done that...'"

Later on, as he travelled in his car, he passed by what he calls his dream vehicle. He got a closer look and saw the licence plate that answered all his questions! It clearly said, "I did..."

When Colin returned home from his business trip, he told his wife about what had happened and she responded with, "Well then, go and do it. Don't just talk about it!"

He decided to go out and order his own personalized plates that said "I DID," so that way he could begin to live the dream.

Every time someone asks him what "I DID" means, he tells them the story. From that moment on, he has worked at building a business that could help others unlock their potential and achieve their dreams simply by acting on whatever it is that lies ahead of them. He believes that the key to making this happen is born into every person.

As we sat over coffee, Colin went on to say that his company understands that each and every person—regardless of age, gender, race, and religion—has a story to tell, from working in the home, to having a corner office in a palatial tower. Perhaps you were born with advantages or disadvantages physically or mentally; maybe you are a professional athlete or a rock star. Every person has a story that resonates with someone, somewhere, somehow. His company—called "I Did Consulting Services Ltd." operating as "I DID" (www.idid.ca)—challenges people to unlock and unleash their story, whether it is educational, spiritual, medical, career-related, personal, about fitness, weight gain and/ or loss, or an athletic or sports story. He and his company want to hear about it; they want to know, "What is your 'I DID'?" On one of the company's advertisements, it says "MAKE A MOVE or MAKE EXCUSES."

Throughout this past year, Colin has remained true to the statement that he wrote on that airplane. He has encouraged me and helped me with anything that I ask for, without fail. He feels, and I totally agree with him, that this story about my personal journey will make a great chapter in his book.

Isn't that what all of this is about anyway? If we look, and we don't really need to look that hard, we can easily find victims who are connecting with each other from a place of misery. They share war wounds with each other and seemingly try to compete for who has the worst childhood experiences.

I say, "Enough of that! It is time to begin the healing journey." To me, wallowing in the depths of our despair is much like giving our abusers the chance to continue their reign of terror over our adult lives when they have already terrorized our childhoods. Now is the time to take a step, and then when you are ready, take another step and so on toward living your life to the fullest and helping someone else up out of the darkness. It is not important how big that step is, it is only important that you take it.

Whether the step is letting your loved ones know what has happened to you, starting therapy, finding your voice, or simply shredding that big bag of shame that has burdened you for so long, it doesn't matter so long as you do it. So many of us who have kept our abuse a secret for the majority of our lives think of ourselves as weak. Nothing could be further from the truth— we are strong, we are smart, we are brave, and we are not alone anymore.

Now that this part of my journey is over, I can look back and say, "I DID write this book and shred my shame." Now, I will set my mind to my next "I DID," and I challenge you to do the same.

Peace, love, and VICTOR!

THE TAKEAWAY LESSON

All big changes, large goals reached, and incredible dreams that have come true started with taking one tiny step in the right direction. Take your step today. It counts more than you will ever know.

Postscript

It is almost one year ago today that I first experienced the relief that came from shredding the shame that I had been carrying since childhood. As that chapter of my life comes to a close, I look forward very much to what is coming next. If my past is any indication of what the future holds, I am sure to be in for another wild ride.

As a young child, the most devastating effect that my abuse had on me was how it made me feel so very alone. Somehow that feeling of being alone spilled over into the rest of my experiences and I was left with very poor self-esteem. That poor self-esteem made it hard for me to accept that I was worthy of having good things happen to me and of having healthy relationships.

Through my own hard work and determination, I was able to change that old view of myself. What I failed to realize was that I actually had already accomplished some really great things in my life and had overcome so many obstacles. Someone who was weak and suffering did not make those accomplishments: a very strong and powerful young woman made them. All I had needed was a small push forward and a good hard look in the mirror.

At the point in my life when the Victor Walk took place, I had already dealt with much of my pain and was well on my way to healing. The Victor Walk for me was the final piece of the puzzle and I hadn't even realized I was missing it. In order for me to move forward with confidence, I needed to feel the power of Shredding the Shame. I needed to accept that I did not need anyone else's approval for how I moved forward. I did not need anything more than the positive attitude and determined spirit I already had; they had gotten me through life's toughest moments.

I would like to help you find your power, release your shame, and dare to dream about the amazing future that is yours to create. You are complete just the way you are and sometimes all we need to do is let go of the thing that no longer serves us, the shame.

Author Biography

Kelli Benis was born in Calgary, Alberta and grew up in Lethbridge, Alberta, where she currently lives. Raised by loving parents, she was the younger of two children and was sexually abused by her grandfather from the age of four until twelve. Cloaked in the silence of shame, she kept her secret for twenty years before she was able to find the courage to tell her immediate family in an effort to ensure her children would not be exposed to her abuser.

It would be another twenty years before Benis was able to tell her story to the world—fuelled by the inspiration provided by attending the Victor Walk on May 23, 2013 on the steps of Parliament Hill with Theo Fleury, the former NHL player who is also a survivor of childhood abuse.

Benis is passionate about inspiring others to come forward and find their voices in the hope of raising awareness about this issue, which thrives in an atmosphere of silence. She continues to seek out opportunities to share her story so that others may also enjoy living their lives free from the shackles of shame. She is motivated by the heartfelt belief that the more we connect with each other through our adversities and support each other in overcoming them, the more connected we will be as a community.

Kelli Benis: Motivational & Inspirational Speaker

Kelli Benis talks about her personal journey of healing from the trauma of child sexual abuse. In her presentations, audiences hear the powerful and moving story about how she was able to shred the shame she felt by finding her voice. Using her experiences as an example, she encourages others to find their path to empowerment. Benis shares how her early experience of abuse spilled over into the rest of her life, long after the abuse ended. She highlights the importance of recognizing the side effects that abuse in our childhood can have on us and what we can do, as we grow older, to take charge of our own personal outcomes.

How Long Is It?

The presentation is approximately one hour long but can be modified.

Who Will It Help?

Benis can tailor her presentations to suit various audiences. Her story resonates with many people who, for various reasons, are struggling with their own issues (such as childhood trauma and addiction) and are ashamed to ask for help. Benis provides insight into the fact that some of the problems we face today are an overflow of what we endured when we were younger. Many will find relief in simply knowing that they are not alone in their struggles and hopefully will be inspired to seek out help.

Lasting Inspiration

The single most beneficial aspect of Benis' talk is that it provides the audience hope, rooted in real life experiences. Benis communicates the inspirational message that despair is temporary and that we are all stronger than we believe.

For Questions and Bookings:
www.KelliBenis.com

Twitter:
@kbenis1

Facebook:
www.facebook.com/shreddingshame

If you want to get on the path to be a published author by
Influence Publishing please go to
www.InfluencePublishing.com

Inspiring books that influence change

More information on our other titles and how to submit your
own proposal can be found at
www.InfluencePublishing.com